International Trade
and the
Montreal Protocol

Research by the Energy and Environmental Programme is supported by generous contributions of finance and technical advice from the following:

British Nuclear Fuels • British Gas • British Petroleum
Department of Trade and Industry • Eastern Group
Enron Europe • Enterprise Oil • Esso • LASMO
Mitsubishi Fuels • National Grid • National Power
Nuclear Electric • PowerGen • Saudi Aramco • Shell
Statoil • Texaco • Tokyo Electric Power Company

Additional support is received for specific research projects from the following:

Commission of the European Communities
Chubu Electric Power Co • UK Department of Environment
ENEL • Energy Technology Support Unit
German Environment Ministry • Hydro-Quebec
Imatran Voima Oy • Japan National Oil Company
London Electricity • Rolls Royce Industrial Power
Siemens • Southern Electric • Swiss Environment Ministry
Tennessee Valley Authority

International Trade
and the
Montreal Protocol

Duncan Brack

THE ROYAL INSTITUTE OF
INTERNATIONAL AFFAIRS
Energy and Environmental Programme
International Economics Programme

EARTHSCAN
Earthscan Publications Ltd, London

First published in Great Britain in 1996 by

Royal Institute of International Affairs, 10 St James's Square, London SW1Y 4LE

(Charity Registration No. 208 223) and Earthscan Publications Ltd,

120 Pentonville Road, London N1 9JN

Distributed in North America by

The Brookings Institution, 1775 Massachusetts Avenue NW,

Washington DC 20036-2188

A catalogue record for this book is available from the British Library.

ISBN 1 85383 345 2

Earthscan Publications Limited is an editorially independent subsidiary of Kogan Page Limited and publishes in association with the International Institute of Environment and Development and the World Wide Fund for Nature.

Printed and bound by Biddles Limited, Guildford and King's Lynn.

Cover by Visible Edge.

Cover illustration by Andy Lovel.

Contents

Tables

Figures

Boxes

Preface

Debate over the relationship between trade liberalization and environmental protection is hardly new. It received attention at the Stockholm UN Conference on the Human Environment in 1972, and by then the General Agreement on Tariffs and Trade (GATT) had already established a committee on the issue. But that committee, and the debate, remained relatively quiescent for the following two decades despite the steady growth of environmental law. However, the Rio 'Earth Summit' of 1992; the completion of the Uruguay Round of the GATT and associated establishment of the World Trade Organization (WTO); and the controversies surrounding the infamous US–Mexico tuna-dolphin disputes, the international hardwood trade, and auto fuel efficiency standards combined to raise the profile and level of concern to unprecedented levels in the 1990s.

Given this historical background, combined with the intrinsic importance of the topic, two of RIIA's research programmes – International Economics (IEP) and Energy and Environmental (EEP) – decided jointly to appoint a researcher to conduct and oversee research on the topic.

In developing a joint research programme, we have been guided by our belief that the most interesting and important questions lie not so much in the relatively well-trodden economic theory of the topic, but rather in the specific issues raised by actual environmental problems and regimes. We are concerned with the institutional and political realities that international environmental policy and the world's trading regimes must face as they mature and grapple with real-world problems and vested interests. Hence the project was conceived as a series of in-depth studies on very specific empirical topics.

The Montreal Protocol on Substances that Deplete the Ozone Layer was a natural choice as the first of these studies, owing both to the intrinsic importance of the ozone problem and its salience as an illustration of the crucial broader issues surrounding the relationship between multilateral environmental agreements and the world's trading systems. The Montreal Protocol has been widely hailed as the great success story of environmental diplomacy in the 1980s, establishing a regime that has evolved rapidly over time, in response to developing scientific knowledge, to the point of enforcing controls at a level that appeared inconceivable a decade ago. One significant feature of the Protocol is its trade provisions. Yet as the Montreal Protocol moves from the realm of rule-making to implementation, concerns about the regime have grown.

Duncan Brack's study provides the first detailed appraisal of the political, economic, and institutional role of the Protocol's trade provisions, and the problems that still remain to be tackled in implementation, enforcement, and extension of commitments to developing countries. Brack concludes that the trade provisions, which transgress the guiding principles of non-discrimination embodied in the GATT, were both essential to the successful development of the regime and justified by the multilateral nature of the agreement and the requirements of realpolitik. But illegal production and trade remain an Achilles' heel of the regime, potentially undermining both the confidence of industries that have 'played by the rules' and invested in alternatives to CFCs and the legal structures relating to the participation of former Soviet states and the potential extension of commitments to developing countries.

Brack's study presents a clear and incisive overview of the development of the Montreal Protocol regime, from its inception in 1987 to the Vienna conference of December 1995. It illustrates not only the considerable success of the Protocol and its trade provisions, but the pitfalls that still threaten it. It is also rich in lessons for other existing and potential multilateral environmental agreements, and for some of the areas that may be addressed at the December 1996 WTO ministerial meeting in Singapore and in subsequent multilateral trade negotiations. In bringing such a complex and sensitive study to a successful conclusion, Duncan Brack has displayed a real gift for explaining difficult topics in clear and accessible language. Over the course of his brief tenure at RIIA, he has established himself as a highly valued member of the research staff and a widely cited expert in the increasingly important area of trade and the environment.

IEP would like to express its sincere thanks to the Ford Foundation, which funded part of this research under the aegis of a wider project covering post-Uruguay Round trade issues. Regrettably, neither of the two environmental institutions that had originally expressed an intention to support the work in the end did so, but the success of the project vindicates EEP's decision to pursue the joint research by drawing on the Programme's core industrial and foundation funds, for which we are eternally grateful.

Duncan Brack will now be proceeding to a shorter study on trade and competitiveness aspects of energy efficiency standards. Other identified topics for the series, conditional upon obtaining project funding, would span analysis of the Basel regime on the international waste trade, trade aspects of eco-labelling, and competitiveness aspects of energy taxation and border tax adjustments. We hope and expect that this series will make a significant intellectual contribution to the widening debate on trade and the environment.

April 1996

Dr Michael Grubb
Head, Energy and Environmental Programme

Dr Benn Steil
Head, International Economics Programme

Acknowledgments

A large number of people were enormously helpful to me in the preparation of this report. I would particularly like to thank Vic Buxton (Environment Canada), James Cameron (FIELD), Nick Campbell (ICI Klea), Steve Charnovitz (Global Environment and Trade Study), Tom Duafala (Methyl Bromide Global Coalition), Richard Eglin (WTO), Owen Greene (Bradford University), Veena Jha (UNCTAD), Jean Lamont (DTI), Tom Land (US EPA), Peter Landymore (ODA), Steve Lee-Bapty (DoE), Rachel Lewis, Jim Losey (formerly US EPA), Mack Macfarland (UNEP), Trish MacQuarrie (Environment Canada), Brendan Murphy (HM Customs & Excise), Sebastien Oberthür (Free University Berlin), Hermann Ott (Wuppertal Institute), Martin Porter (University of Bath), Madhava Sarma (UNEP Ozone Secretariat), Hugo-Maria Schally (Montreal Protocol Implementation Committee), Vivian Sheridan (DuPont External Affairs), Rob Shooter (ODA), Robert van Slooten (DTI), David Stirpe (Alliance for Responsible Atmospheric Policy), Patrick Széll (DoE), John Temple Lang (European Commission), Geoff Tierney (DoE), Tony Vogelsberg (DuPont Chemicals), Halina Ward (FIELD) and Tom Werkema (Elf Atochem). Others, too numerous to mention, who attended the Chatham House study group in December 1995 made many valuable contributions. UNEP's Ozone Secretariat kindly provided me with papers and access to meetings. At Chatham House, Jane Chapman and Hannah Doe ensured that the book was produced both professionally and on time, despite my attempts to delay it, and my two programme heads, Benn Steil and – especially – Michael Grubb provided essential oversight and guidance at all times. Full responsibility for the final text of course remains with me.

April 1996   Duncan Brack

Abbreviations

CEITs	countries with economies in transition
CFCs	chlorofluorocarbons
CITES	Convention on International Trade in Endangered Species
EPA	(US) Environmental Protection Agency
GATT	General Agreement on Tariffs and Trade
GEF	Global Environment Facility
HBFCs	hydrobromofluorocarbons
HCFCs	hydrochlorofluorocarbons
HFCs	hydrofluorocarbons
IPR	inward processing relief
IRS	(US) Internal Revenue Service
MACS	mobile air-conditioning systems
MEA	multilateral environmental agreement
NAFTA	North American Free Trade Agreement
NGO	non-governmental organization
ODP	ozone-depleting potential
ODS	ozone-depleting substances
OECD	Organization for Economic Cooperation and Development
PPMs	process and production methods
TBT	(GATT Agreement on) Technical Barriers to Trade
TEAP	Technology and Economic Assessment Panel
UNCTAD	United Nations Conference on Trade and Development
UNDP	United Nations Development Programme
UNEP	United Nations Environment Programme
UNIDO	United Nations Industrial Development Organization
UV	ultraviolet
WMO	World Meteorological Organization
WTO	World Trade Organization

Summary

This report examines the interaction between international trade and environmental protection in the context of the Montreal Protocol on Substances that Deplete the Ozone Layer. The Protocol is one of the most effective multilateral environmental agreements (MEAs) currently in existence. It has achieved almost universal participation and a progressive development of ever more stringent control schedules on ozone-depleting substances (ODS) in response to developing scientific and technological knowledge.

The trade provisions of the agreement

The trade provisions of the Protocol, which require restrictions on trade between parties and non-parties to the agreement, form an important and distinctive element. The key conclusion of this study is that these provisions were a vital component in (a) building the wide international coverage the treaty has achieved and (b) preventing industrial migration to non-parties to escape the controls on ODS.

The provisions potentially violate the non-discrimination principles of the General Agreement on Tariffs and Trade (GATT). Trade restrictions which would have been less GATT-inconsistent, however, were not practicable, and the possibility of a legal challenge under the GATT both undermines the credibility of the ozone regime and inhibits the negotiation of similar provisions in future MEAs. Amendment of the GATT to remove the possibility of challenges to such trade restrictions is therefore required.

Developing countries

The trade provisions were necessary but not sufficient to encourage developing countries to participate in the ozone regime; financial support and technology transfer were also essential. Problems have been caused, however, for trade in ODS and in products containing ODS by the differential phase-out schedules of developing and industrialized countries. The provision of additional finance would ameliorate these problems by permitting faster phase-out. Licensing and monitoring systems would help control the 'dumping' of obsolete products and technology in developing countries.

Non-compliance and illegal trade

New problems now threaten the effectiveness of the Montreal Protocol. Non-compliance with phase-out obligations by some parties calls the treaty's non-compliance procedures into question, and will require the provision of financial and technical assistance to remove the problem at source. The growing problem of illegal trade in ODS cannot be tackled successfully by environment ministries and institutions acting alone; coordinated action with trade and industry ministries and enforcement agencies, such as police and customs, is also required.

Lessons for the future

MEAs such as the Montreal Protocol offer the best way forward in striking an appropriate balance between the sometimes conflicting objectives of trade liberalization and environmental sustainability. Future MEAs dealing with the control of substances causing transboundary environmental damage may need to incorporate trade provisions similar to those of the Montreal Protocol. The problems which the ozone regime has experienced – with the GATT, differential phase-outs, non-compliance and illegal trade – should therefore be anticipated and resolved.

Chapter 1

International trade and the environment

In recent years the interaction between international trade and environmental protection has generated much debate, but little consensus.[1] The international community is in theory committed *both* to trade liberalization, through the Uruguay Round extension of the General Agreement on Tariffs and Trade (GATT) and the creation of the World Trade Organization (WTO), *and* to environmentally sustainable development, through the agreements signed at the UN Conference on Environment and Development, the 'Earth Summit' of 1992.

In theory, the pursuit of the two objectives should be entirely compatible. According to the theory of comparative advantage, trade allows countries to specialize in the production of goods and services in which they are relatively most efficient. In other words, trade enables countries to maximize output from a given input of resources – which is a movement in the direction of environmental sustainability. Furthermore, trade liberalization can help to remove distortionary subsidies and pricing policies, improving the efficiency of resource allocation, and encourage the spread of environmentally friendly technology. The higher rate of growth of income resulting from trade also helps to generate the resources needed for investment in environmental protection (though this is not an automatic link; appropriate environmental policies need to be pursued simultaneously).

Given modern systems of economic activity, however, trade can also harm the environment. To the extent that environmental externalities are not incorporated into economic prices and decision-making, trade can act to magnify unsustainable patterns of economic activity, exacerbating

---

[1] For a fuller discussion of these issues, see in particular Duncan Brack, 'Balancing trade and the environment', *International Affairs* 71:3, July 1995; Steve Charnovitz, 'Free trade, fair trade, green trade: defogging the debate', *Cornell International Law Journal* 27:3, Summer 1994; and Dan Esty, *Greening the GATT: Trade, Environment and the Future* (Washington, DC: Institute for International Economics, 1994).

problems of pollution and resource depletion. Where externalities *are* being incorporated (through environmental taxation, for example, or regulation), the process is invariably proceeding at different speeds in different countries. Yet trade rules are set internationally, and the current GATT regulations may fail to allow for such differences in national efforts at achieving environmental sustainability, even where policies are aimed at controlling transboundary or global environmental problems. In addition, a country with strict environmental regulations may fear that its economy will be undermined by competition from other countries with more lax environmental standards (and hence potentially lower production costs).

Trade and environmental policies are therefore inextricably interlinked. Conflict between trade liberalization and environmental protection has already erupted in a number of instances as regulations drawn up in pursuit of the objective of environmental sustainability have been challenged as erecting barriers to trade. Among the better-known examples from the last ten years are the US–Mexico tuna-dolphin disputes (where the provisions of the US Marine Mammal Protection Act were deployed in an attempt to reduce dolphin kills associated with tuna fishing); the US–EU disagreement over US imports of European cars which failed to comply with the US CAFE (corporate average fuel economy) fuel efficiency standards; and the intra-EU dispute over the Danish government's regulations requiring carbonated drinks to be sold in containers with a deposit and return system.

One of the major foundations of the GATT agreement is a hostility to unilateral action on the part of WTO members. Finding against the US ban on imports of tuna from Mexico in the 1991 tuna-dolphin dispute, the GATT disputes panel commented that to accept the US case would be to agree that each GATT member 'could unilaterally determine the life or health protection policies from which other contracting parties could not deviate without jeopardising their rights under the [GATT]'.[2] The essential ethos of the GATT, drawn up after the Second World War against stark memories of the protectionism and collapsing trade of the 1930s, is *proscriptive:* states must be prevented from erecting barriers to the free

---

[2] US: Restrictions on Tuna (1991): Report of the Panel, para. 5.27.

flow of goods. This principle lies in uneasy counterpoint to the necessarily *prescriptive* nature of environmental protection, which generally requires particular actions on the part of governments.

It is not surprising, therefore, that one of the major mechanisms often proposed for the reconciliation of trade liberalization and environmental protection is the negotiation of multilateral action, which avoids unilateral trade-disrupting measures while at the same time almost certainly proving more effective in tackling transboundary or global environmental problems. More than 180 multilateral environmental agreements (MEAs) already exist, of which about 20 incorporate trade measures. These include three of the most important: the Basel Convention on hazardous waste, the Convention on International Trade in Endangered Species (CITES), and the Montreal Protocol on ozone-depleting substances. In the absence of any comprehensive framework of global environmental law, the negotiation of further MEAs – such as the protocol to the Climate Change Convention currently under discussion – will form an increasingly prominent part of the international agenda.

The interaction of MEAs with the international trading system is therefore an important area of discussion. The April 1994 agreement formally concluding the Uruguay Round of the GATT agreed to establish a Committee on Trade and Environment of the new World Trade Organization, taking forward the work begun under an earlier GATT group. The Committee aims to 'identify the relationship between trade measures and environmental measures, in order to promote sustainable development' and 'to make appropriate recommendations on whether any modifications of the provisions of the multilateral trading system are required, compatible with the open, equitable and non-discriminatory nature of the system'.[3] The Committee's work programme includes a review of 'the relationship between the provisions of the multilateral trading system and trade measures for environmental purposes, including those pursuant to multilateral environmental agreements'. It is due to report with recommendations to the WTO ministerial meeting in Singapore in December 1996.

---

[3] World Trade Organization, trade and environment decision of 14 April 1994.

The purpose of the Trade and Environment project of the Royal Institute of International Affairs is to examine actual areas of conflict and interaction between trade liberalization and environmental protection and to contribute to the debate over their future development and resolution. This paper, the first in a series of reports, addresses the following issues with regard to one of the best-known and most effective MEAs, the 1987 Montreal Protocol on Substances that Deplete the Ozone Layer:

- What are the Protocol's trade provisions, why were they negotiated and how have they evolved?
- Have they proved effective in achieving their original aims, and how important have they been in achieving the overall objectives of the Protocol?
- Are they compatible with international trade agreements?
- How effectively have they been enforced, and what challenges do they now face?

This is not merely a theoretical discussion. Over the next few years, the depletion of the Earth's stratospheric ozone layer as a result of emissions of industrial chemicals will reach its peak. Its recovery depends on the effectiveness of the regime established by the Montreal Protocol. To the extent that the trade provisions of the Protocol contributed to the impact of the ozone regime, they will provide a valuable model for future MEAs designed to tackle similar problems of environmental degradation.

Chapter 2

Protecting the ozone layer

2.1 The holes in the layer[4]

Ozone trends

Ozone is a molecule comprising three oxygen atoms. Comparatively rare in the Earth's atmosphere, 90% is found in the stratospheric 'ozone layer', between 10 and 50 km (6–30 miles) above the Earth's surface. It absorbs all but a small fraction of the biologically active ultraviolet radiation (UV-B; radiation of wavelength 280–310 nm) emanating from the sun. Plant and animal life on the Earth's surface is thus protected from UV-B, which in high doses can be particularly damaging to natural organisms. The absorption of UV-B by the ozone layer also creates a source of heat, playing a key role in the temperature structure of the atmosphere.

Concern began to be expressed in the early 1970s that the ozone layer was vulnerable to damage by the emission into the atmosphere of chemicals known as halocarbons, compounds containing various combinations of chlorine, fluorine, bromine, carbon and hydrogen. The most common ozone-depleting substances were thought to be the family of chlorofluorocarbons, or CFCs, first produced in Belgium in 1892, and discovered, by General Motors chemists in the US in 1929, to be an effective heat transfer fluid. Stable and non-toxic, CFCs came to be used for refrigeration, air-conditioning and blowing foams, as solvents, sterilants and aerosol propellants. Major new uses were found for CFCs each decade, and world production, concentrated largely in the US and western Europe, doubled

---

[4] Information in this section is largely taken from *Scientific Assessment of Ozone Depletion: 1994* (Nairobi: UNEP, 1994); *Environmental Effects of Ozone Depletion: 1994 Assessment* (Nairobi: UNEP, 1994); and Edward A. Parson, 'Protecting the ozone layer', in Peter M. Haas, Robert O. Keohane and Marc A. Levy (eds), *Institutions for the Earth* (Cambridge, MA / London: MIT Press, 1993).

roughly every five years until 1970. Halons, related chemicals containing bromine, were used as effective, non-toxic and non-corrosive fire extinguishants.

A possible mechanism for the depletion of the ozone layer by CFCs was first published in 1974 and was reinforced by further research. As CFCs are so stable, when released into the lower atmosphere they persist long enough to diffuse across the boundary into the stratosphere, where they are broken apart by solar UV radiation to release chlorine atoms, which react very strongly with ozone molecules. The chlorine oxide which is formed then undergoes further reactions which regenerate the original chlorine, allowing the process to be repeated many times; each chlorine atom can destroy an estimated 100,000 ozone molecules before it is removed from the stratosphere. Although ozone is continually recreated from oxygen by UV radiation, the presence of chlorine speeds up ozone destruction but not its creation, reducing the equilibrium concentration of ozone. Similar reactions take place between bromine and ozone.

These reactions are particularly intense within the polar stratospheric clouds that form above Antarctica in the extremely cold night of the southern hemisphere winter. Reactions which occur on the surfaces of ice and aerosol particles within the clouds release chlorine and bromine in active forms that accumulate in the polar vortex. When the sun rises in the spring they break apart, under sunlight and low temperatures, to release active chlorine and bromine which rapidly destroy ozone. This accelerated process stops when the temperature rises and the vortex breaks up. The result is the 'ozone hole', an area of sharp decline in ozone concentrations over most of Antarctica for about two months during the southern hemisphere spring. Stratospheric air above the Arctic is generally warmer and less confined than over the Antarctic, and fewer clouds form there; thus Arctic ozone depletion is less severe. Polar ozone depletion is accelerated by atmospheric circulation, which tends to move CFCs in the stratosphere away from the tropics towards both poles.

Observations of stratospheric ozone concentrations since the 1970s have confirmed the evidence of gradual ozone depletion with seasonal variations. Since 1979, ozone concentrations have fallen by about 4% per decade at mid-latitudes (30°–60°) in both the northern and southern hemispheres, the losses being largest during the winter and spring.[5] In the spring of 1995, stratospheric ozone levels over Europe were 10–12% lower than in the mid-1970s, and over North America 5–10% lower, although at times as much as 20% lower in some places.[6] The tropics (20°N–20°S) experienced little or no ozone depletion. In contrast, the Antarctic ozone holes of 1992 and 1993 were the most severe on record, with ozone being depleted by more than 99% (i.e. no ozone was detected at all) at altitudes of 14–19 km in October 1992 and 1993. It is believed that sulphate aerosols from the volcanic eruption at Mount Pinatubo in 1991 accelerated ozone destruction,[7] and the ozone hole of 1994 was no worse than that of the previous year. The 1995 ozone hole, though neither the deepest nor the largest on record, proved of longest duration, covering an area greater than 10 million km^2 (roughly equivalent to the surface area of Europe) for 77 days, compared to a previous high of 63 days in 1993, and just 25 days in 1985; it was larger than 20 million km^2 on 39 days.[8]

Ozone losses above the Arctic have been lower, with a total loss of about 10–20% compared to 1979. The Arctic winter of 1994–5, however, was exceptionally cold, and measurements of total ozone in the polar vortex in March 1995 were 20–30% below normal. On individual days when the vortex rotated to cover Siberia, total ozone fell by a record 35% in particular locations.[9] The winter of 1995–6 was even colder, and ozone concentrations over Britain fell by almost 50% in the first week in March, the lowest levels ever recorded over the UK.[10] It is suspected that this

[5] 4.3% in the northern, and 4.1% in the southern, hemisphere: *Journal of Geophysical Research* 100, 20 December 1995, pp. 25,867–76.

[6] World Meteorological Organization (WMO) press briefing, 15 February 1995, reported in *Global Environmental Change Report* VII:4, 24 February 1995, p. 5.

[7] Research suggests, however, that volcanic eruptions will only contribute to ozone depletion in conditions of high chlorine loading; where chlorine levels are low, sulphur dioxide may actually contribute to ozone formation. See *Geophysical Research Letters* 22, 15 November 1995, pp. 3,035–8.

[8] WMO figures, reported in *Global Environmental Change Report* VII:24, 22 December 1995, p. 5.

[9] SESAME (Second European Stratospheric Arctic and Midlatitude Experiment) figures, reported in *Global Environmental Change Report* VII:19, 6 October 1995, p. 6.

[10] Met Office figures, reported in *The Independent,* 8 March 1996, p. 1 (Nicholas Schoon, 'Hole in ozone threatens UK').

unexpected recurrence of cold winter temperatures in the stratosphere may itself be due to cumulative ozone destruction, or possibly to climate change; in either case, ozone depletion over the northern hemisphere may be more severe for the next few years than anticipated.[11]

The impact of ozone depletion

Depletion of the ozone layer means that more UV-B radiation can reach the surface of the Earth. Lack of historical data coupled with the effects of clouds and pollution have made modelling difficult, but clear-sky obser-vations of levels of UV-B so far fit in quite well with the theories. Large increases have been observed in southern high latitudes in connection with the Antarctic ozone holes. Measurements at Palmer Station (64°S) in springtime show higher levels of radiation than at the distinctly sunnier San Diego (32°N). In 1992–3, large increases in UV-B were measured at northern middle and high latitudes, the first reported examples of persis-tent increases over densely populated regions. The data suggest that UV-B levels were about 8–10% higher in 1994 than 15 years earlier at 45°N and S (the latitude of Ottawa and Venice in the northern, and Dunedin in the southern, hemisphere), with higher levels towards the poles, particularly in the south. Increases in clear-sky UV-B are predicted to climb to 15% in northern mid-latitudes in winter and spring (8% at other times), and 13% in southern mid-latitudes, at the peak of ozone depletion around the turn of the century. Levels in specific locations can be even higher, particularly as the area of ozone depletion around the poles sometimes rotates to cover populated areas. In southern South America in 1992, a doubling of UV-B radiation was experienced following a 50% fall in ozone. Significantly higher than normal levels of solar UV were observed at ground level in the UK in February and March 1996.[12]

Increased penetration of UV-B radiation has adverse effects on human health, animals, plants, micro-organisms, materials and air quality. In

[11] Fred Pearce, 'Big freeze digs a deeper hole in ozone layer', *New Scientist,* 16 March 1996, p. 7.
[12] WMO and UK National Radiological Protection Board announcements, reported in the *Financial Times,* 13 March 1996, p. 4 (Clive Cookson, 'UV radiation hits record high level in northern world').

humans, chronic exposure to UV-B is clearly associated with the risk of eye damage: a 1% increase in stratospheric ozone depletion is estimated to result in a potential 0.6–0.8% rise in the incidence of cataracts (100,000–150,000 additional cases worldwide). UV-B radiation can induce suppression of immune systems; the importance of this is unknown but may be significant in areas where infectious diseases are common or immune functions already impaired. In light-skinned populations, exposure to UV-B radiation is the key risk factor in the development of squamous and basal cell (non-melanoma) skin cancer; experiments suggest that its incidence increases by 2% for every 1% reduction in stratospheric ozone. The risk of the more serious melanoma also may increase with UV-B exposure, particularly during childhood, though the mechanism is not well understood; melanoma is now one of the more common cancers among white-skinned people.[13]

Animals are subject to similar effects of increased UV-B. In addition, aquatic ecosystems are particularly vulnerable to UV-B, a matter of some concern not least because more than 30% of the world's animal protein for human consumption comes from the sea. UV-B damages the early developmental stages of fish, shrimp, crab and amphibians and reduces the productivity of phytoplankton, the foundation of aquatic food webs. Situated primarily at high latitudes and therefore particularly exposed to the impact of ozone loss, it has been estimated that phytoplankton could suffer a loss of 5% in numbers as a result of a 16% level of ozone depletion, a reduction which translates into a loss of about 7 million tonnes of fish per year. Plant growth may also be directly reduced by UV-B radiation, resulting in decreased crop yields and quality, and damage to forests. Reductions in the productivity of marine and terrestrial ecosystems could in turn reduce the uptake of carbon dioxide, thus contributing to climate change.

Synthetic polymers, such as plastics and rubber, and naturally occurring biopolymers, such as wood, are adversely affected by UV-B; the damage caused ranges from discoloration to loss of mechanical integrity. Increases

---

[13] The second most prevalent tumour in US males aged 30–49 and the fourth most prevalent in males aged 50–59, cited in Seth Cagin and Philip Dray, *Between Earth and Sky: How CFCs Changed our World and Endangered the Ozone Layer* (New York: Pantheon, 1993).

in UV-B may either limit the lifetimes of these materials or cause a need for more expensive production processes. Finally, reductions in stratospheric ozone and the accompanying increases in UV-B radiation have important effects on the troposphere, the lower region of the atmosphere. Its chemical reactivity changes, increasing both production and destruction of ozone, which at low levels is both directly toxic and a key component of smog. Changes in the concentrations of other oxidants may also affect the atmospheric lifetimes of climatically important gases such as methane or CFC substitutes. These processes are still not fully understood, but indicate the possibility of complex relationships between stratospheric ozone reduction, tropospheric chemistry and climate change.

2.2 Ozone diplomacy[14]

While the first major statement of scientific concern over ozone depletion came in 1974,[15] convincing evidence was not available until 1985, with the publication of the 'ozone hole' paper by members of the British Antarctic Survey.[16] Even then, neither the magnitude of the problem nor its causes (the linkage between CFCs and ozone destruction) became apparent until 1988, with the release of the report of the Ozone Trends Panel reviewing evidence particularly from US Antarctic expeditions in 1986 and 1987.[17]

[14] Information in this section, and in sections 2.3–2.5, is largely taken from Richard Benedick, *Ozone Diplomacy: New Directions in Safeguarding the Planet* (Cambridge, MA/ London: Harvard University Press, 1991); Tony Brenton, *The Greening of Machiavelli: The Evolution of International Environmental Politics* (London: Royal Institute of International Affairs / Earthscan, 1994); Parson, 'Protecting the ozone layer'; and Caroline Thomas, *The Environment in International Relations* (London: Royal Institute of International Affairs, 1992).

[15] M. J. Molina and F. S. Rowland, 'Stratospheric sink for chlorofluoromethanes: chlorine atom catalysed destruction of ozone', *Nature* 249, 1974, pp. 810–14. Mario Molina and Sherwood Rowland, along with Paul Crutzen, were awarded the 1995 Nobel Prize for Chemistry in recognition of their work on ozone depletion.

[16] J. C. Farman, B. G. Gardiner and J. D. Shanklin, 'Large losses of total ozone in Antarctica reveal seasonal ClOx/NOx interaction', *Nature* 315, 1985, pp. 207–10. Subsequent re-examination of satellite observations from the late 1970s supported the findings.

[17] National Aeronautics and Space Administration, 'Executive Summary of the Ozone Trends Panel' (Washington, DC: NASA, 15 March 1988). The full report was not published until 1991.

The early stages of international action were therefore characterized by agreements merely to cooperate over research. A research-oriented 'World Plan of Action on the Ozone Layer' was agreed in 1977, with the Coordinating Committee on the Ozone Layer, containing experts from agencies and non-governmental organizations (NGOs), established by the United Nations Environment Programme (UNEP) to oversee it.

Action in the US had proceeded somewhat further, spurred by earlier debates over the impact on the ozone layer of nitrogen oxide emissions from supersonic aircraft. An effective public campaign resulted in regulations prohibiting the use of CFCs as aerosol propellants in non-essential applications by 1978; this was observed by Canada, Sweden and Norway. US production of CFC-11 and -12 fell from 46% of the world total in 1974 to 28% by 1985 as a result; alternative propellants were rapidly introduced and often proved more economic than the original CFCs. European Community governments were less convinced by the (then uncertain) state of the evidence, and preferred to introduce controls on total production rather than to apply use controls in single sectors. European environmental groups, concentrating at the time on the issue of acid rain, proved less effective in campaigning on ozone depletion than their US counterparts. In 1980 the EC agreed to freeze production capacity of CFC-11 and -12 and reduce their use in aerosols by at least 30% from 1976 levels by the end of 1981. After 1982, CFC production in the US started to accelerate once more, as usage increased sharply in the mobile air-conditioning and foam-blowing sectors, arguably showing the wisdom of the EC approach. Since production capacity in the EC was at the time substantially above consumption levels, however, a capacity freeze contributed little to the control of CFC emissions.

Negotiations for an international convention on the ozone layer to regulate CFC production and use, started in 1981, proceeded slowly. While the US and its allies favoured a range of control measures on the use of CFCs in various sectors (originally only aerosols, but others were added later), the EC argued mainly for a cap on existing production capacity. The differences could not be bridged and the Vienna Convention for the Protection of the Ozone Layer, agreed in March 1985, contained pledges only to cooperate in research and monitoring, to share information on CFC production and emissions, and to pass control protocols if and when warranted. Although this was a clear disappointment for the supporters of control schedules, they did manage to achieve a resolution empowering UNEP immediately to convene working group negotiations for a protocol, to be signed if possible in 1987.

The full story of the negotiations on the Montreal Protocol on Substances that Deplete the Ozone Layer has been told elsewhere.[18] By comparison with the protracted negotiations over the Vienna Convention, they proceeded remarkably quickly and achieved far more than was initially thought possible. UNEP played a more active role than hitherto, exploiting the powers it was given by the Convention, NGO activity was greater, the US continued to take an advanced leadership role, and the scientific evidence of ozone depletion, notably the discovery of the Antarctic ozone hole, strengthened the case for action. Since the causes of ozone depletion were still unclear, however, tribute should also be paid to the negotiators' willingness to abide by the precautionary principle (where the environmental threat is considered to be potentially so severe as to warrant action in advance of unequivocal proof of the problem), probably for the first time in a major international negotiation. The resulting agreement was signed on 16 September 1987, featuring 50% cuts from 1986 levels in both production and consumption of the five main CFCs by 1999, with interim reductions. Production and consumption of the three main halons was frozen at 1986 levels from 1993. Although these reductions could be attacked as either too little (if the ozone depletion hypothesis was believed) or too much (if it was not), the agreement marked an important political and psychological breakthrough. Following the Ozone Trends Panel report of March 1988, with its convincing evidence of the linkage between ozone depletion and CFCs, opposition to the principle of controls on ozone-depleting substances largely collapsed. Industry came to accept the necessity of introducing alternatives rather than opposing control measures, and concentrated resources on their development, with the aim of being first in the field with the new substances.

---

[18] Most fully in Benedick, *Ozone Diplomacy*; but see also Fiona McConnell's review of the book in *International Environmental Affairs* 3:4, Autumn 1991, pp. 318–20, for a slightly different view.

An important feature of the Montreal Protocol was the flexibility designed into it to allow for its further development in the light of evolving scientific knowledge and technological developments. Even before it entered into force on 1 January 1989, plans were being made to strengthen its provisions, accelerating the phase-out schedules for the CFCs and halons it specified, and adding further chemicals which possessed ozone-depleting potential. The Protocol has now been subject to a number of sets of *adjustments* (to the control schedules) and *amendments* (adding new chemicals for control, and other new components of the treaty), agreed at the regular meetings of the parties. Its main features are examined in the remainder of this chapter, with the exception of the trade provisions, which are the central concern of this report, and are dealt with separately in Chapter 3.

2.3 Control measures on ozone-depleting substances

At the heart of the Montreal Protocol lie the control measures it imposes on the production and consumption of ozone-depleting substances (ODS). The controlled substances are listed in four annexes to the Protocol (see Box 2.1), and Article 2 defines their respective phase-out schedules. These have been progressively tightened with time through the agreements reached in London (1990), Copenhagen (1992) and Vienna (1995). The evolutionary record of the control measures is set out in Table 2.1.

Total production and consumption of the various controlled substances is calculated by weighting each chemical by its ozone-depleting potential, which is also specified in the annexes.[19] During the phase-out period, countries can choose on which particular chemicals within each group to concentrate their controls – or leave it to the market, which should result in the substances easiest to replace being phased out fastest, as the permitted consumption levels decline. Production is defined as total production minus the amount destroyed by approved technologies minus the amounts

---

[19] For HCFCs, only consumption is controlled, as it was believed that this would encourage faster replacement of CFCs.

Table 2.1: Evolving control measures of the Montreal Protocol: non-Article 5 countries (%)[a]

	Montreal	London	Copenhagen	Vienna
Annex A, Group I: CFCs (CFC-11, 12, 113, 114, 115 – those with the most widespread use) (reference year 1986)				
1989	100	100	100	
1992				
1993	80			
1994			25	
1995		50		
1996			0	
1997		15		
1998	50			
1999				
2000		0		
Annex A, Group II: Halons (1211, 1301, 2402) (reference year 1986)[b]				
1992		100	100	
1993	100			
1994			0	
1995		50		
1996				
1997				
1998				
1999				
2000		0		
Annex B, Group I: Other fully halogenated CFCs (10 substances) (reference year 1989)				
1993		80	80	
1994			25	
1995				
1996			0	
1997		15		
1998				
2000		0		
Annex B, Group II: Carbon tetrachloride (reference year 1989)				
1995		15	15	
1996			0	
1997				
2000		0		

Table 2.1 *(continued)*

	Montreal	London	Copenhagen	Vienna
Annex B, Group III: Methyl chloroform (reference year 1989)				
1993		100	100	
1994			50	
1995		70		
1996			0	
2000		30		
2005		0		
Annex C, Group I: HCFCs (40 substances) (reference year 1989)[c]				
1996			100	
2004			65	
2010			35	
2015			10	
2020			0.5[d]	
2030			0	
Annex C, Group II: HBFCs (34 substances)				
1996			0	
Annex E: Methyl bromide (reference year 1991)[e]				
1995			100	100
2001				75
2005				50
2010				0[f]

[a] Figures shown are consumption and production levels permitted by 1 January of the indicated year, compared to consumption and production levels in the reference year.

[b] 'Other halons' identified by scientists but not in commercial use were identified as possessing ozone-depleting potential. The 1990 London Meeting adopted a resolution calling on parties to refrain from using such substances except where no alternatives were available.

[c] The percentages relate to the sum of the consumption level of HCFCs *plus* 3.1% (reduced to 2.8% at Vienna) of the consumption level of CFCs (Annex A, Group I) in 1989.

[d] The Vienna Meeting agreed that the 0.5% of consumption allowed for the period 2020–2030 would be restricted to use in 'the servicing of refrigeration and air-conditioning equipment existing at that date' (i.e. 2020).

[e] All figures exclude use for quarantine and pre-shipment applications.

[f] Excludes production or consumption for agreed 'critical agricultural uses'.

Box 2.1: Ozone-depleting substances controlled by the Montreal Protocol

Annex	Group	ODS	Main uses
A	I	Main CFCs (11, 12, 113, 114, 115)	Refrigerants, aerosol propellants, foam-blowing agents, solvents
	II	Halons	Fire extinguishants
B	I	Other CFCs	Not in widespread use at time of phase-out
	II	Carbon tetrachloride	Feedstock, process agent, solvent
	III	Methyl chloroform	Solvent, used particularly in metals industry
C	I	HCFCs	'Transitional substances' replacing CFCs (with much lower ozone-depleting potentials)
	II	HBFCs	Not in widespread use at time of phase-out
E		Methyl bromide	Fumigant, pesticide (also released from biomass burning and from oceanic algae)

used as chemical feedstock and process agents.[20] Consumption is defined as production plus imports minus exports.

Parties may transfer all or part of their production limit to other countries (to help overcome economies of scale problems as production diminishes to zero) or even all or part of their consumption limit (for small industrialized consumers only), as long as the total combined production or consumption figures do not exceed the sum of the individual limits. Regional Economic Integration Organizations (a category which currently includes only the EU) are permitted to meet the consumption limits jointly

---

[20] Feedstock is defined as 'a controlled substance that undergoes transformation in a process in which it is entirely converted from its original composition'; a process agent is 'a controlled substance that because of its unique chemical and/or physical properties, is used in a chemical process without being entirely chemically transformed': *Supplement to the 1994 Assessments* (Nairobi: UNEP, March 1995), part II, p. 78. Process agents are currently treated by the Montreal Protocol in the same way as feedstock, but this position will be reviewed in 1997: see Decision VII/10 of the Parties to the Montreal Protocol.

– an essential provision for the EU, which cannot impose internal trade restrictions between member states. Production limits may not be aggregated in this way, but as the industrial rationalization clause allows transfer of production between parties, in practice aggregation does occur, although EU member states must still report data individually. The extent of trade in production quotas is difficult to ascertain because of confidentiality requirements, but seems to have occurred mainly in the EU, where regulations govern rationalization between producers, rather than countries; such rationalization must be notified to the relevant authority, whether national (for producers in the same country) or the Commission (for cross-border rationalization).

The parties agreed in 1992 that imports and exports of recycled and used controlled substances should not be included in the calculation of consumption, as long as the relevant data were fully reported to UNEP.[21] This encouraged the recovery, reclamation and recycling of the large volumes of ODS contained in existing equipment, making early phase-out much easier. It has also, however, created particular problems in the area of illegal trade (see Chapter 6).

After the date at which the control measures specify a zero limit, parties may continue to produce or consume for two purposes (as well as feedstock and process agent use, which is excluded from the calculations). Industrialized countries (i.e. non-Article 5 countries – see section 2.4) are allowed to exceed their production limit by 10% or 15% (depending on the substance and the date) to meet the 'basic domestic needs' of developing countries. Production is also permitted for 'essential uses', which must themselves be agreed by a meeting of the parties. Current essential use exemptions include a range of ODS for laboratory and analytical uses, CFCs for metered dose inhalers for asthma and chronic obstructive pulmonary disease, and methyl chloroform for specific applications in rocket motor manufacturing in the US Space Shuttle and Titan programmes.

---

[21] Decision IV/24 of the Parties to the Montreal Protocol, which reversed the earlier Decision I/12H.

2.4 Developing countries and the Multilateral Fund

Developing countries are treated differently from industrialized countries by the Montreal Protocol: a key feature of the agreement and one subject to much negotiation. While the developing world accounted for only 15% of global ODS consumption in 1986, consumption rates were growing much faster there than in industrialized countries – as much as 20% a year in some cases. India and China together were expected to account for almost 700,000 tonnes of CFC use – a third of total world consumption – by 2008.[22] Article 5 of the Protocol permits a developing country with an annual level of consumption of the controlled substances in Annex A (the original five CFCs and three halons) of less than 0.3 kg per capita at any time before 1 January 1999 to delay for ten years its compliance with the control measures set out in Article 2 'in order to meet its basic domestic needs'.[23] During this grace period, consumption in such 'Article 5 parties' must remain below 0.3 kg per capita for Annex A substances, and 0.2 kg per capita for Annex B substances (other CFCs, carbon tetrachloride and methyl chloroform).

Even with this delay period, developing countries argued that they would need financial assistance with conversion to the new substances and technologies, which in general were expected to be more expensive. As the industrialized world was by that stage resolved to move to complete phase-out of CFCs, participation by developing countries was seen as crucial if the goals of the Protocol were not to be compromised. A key feature of the 1990 London Meeting of the Parties was accordingly the negotiation of a financial and technical assistance clause, which took its place in the Protocol as Article 10. The Multilateral Fund was established to pay the 'agreed incremental costs' of company-level investment projects to reduce or eliminate ODS in Article 5 countries. It operates through four implementing agencies: UNEP, the UN Development Programme (UNDP), the UN Industrial Development Organization

---

[22] *Funding Change: Developing Countries and the Montreal Protocol* (London: Friends of the Earth UK, 1990), pp. 10–11.
[23] Montreal Protocol, Article 5.1.

(UNIDO) and the World Bank.[24] Each Article 5 country, assisted by one of these agencies, prepares a country programme, showing its present and projected use of ODS and identifying detailed opportunities for reduction. The Fund's Executive Committee must approve both the country programmes and subsequent proposals for investment projects and institutional strengthening.

The funding level was set at $160 million for the first three years, 1991–3; this was increased to $240 million on the accession of India and China. A further $510 million was agreed for the period 1994–6, including $55 million carried over unallocated from the first tranche. Industrialized country parties contribute to the Fund according to the standard UN assessment scale, and contributions must be additional to other funding. The Global Environment Facility (GEF), established in 1990 to provide finance for tackling global environmental problems, also covers ozone depletion as one of its areas of work. Duplication of effort is avoided by the expedient of restricting GEF funding to countries with economies in transition (i.e. former Comecon members), while the Multilateral Fund assists developing countries.

Non-Article 5 parties also pledge to ensure that appropriate technology should be made available on 'fair and most favourable conditions' (a compromise with the developing countries' preference for 'preferential and non-commercial' terms). [25] In a carefully worded text, Article 5.5 states that the ability of Article 5 countries to comply with the Protocol's provisions 'will depend upon the effective implementation of the financial cooperation . . . and the transfer of technology' clauses. As the control measures of the Protocol have been successfully implemented, a number of developing countries not originally classified as Article 5 parties (because their ODS use was too high) have reduced consumption below

---

[24] As at November 1995, funds allocated to each of the agencies were as follows: UNEP: $18,037,500 (4% of the total; UNEP has no project implementation role, and concentrates mainly on country programmes for small countries, and information exchange); UNDP: $124,459,552 (30%); UNIDO: $79,489,586 (19%); World Bank: $199,870,724 (47%; the World Bank concentrates on large-scale projects). About a quarter of the totals allocated had actually been disbursed; see *Report of the Executive Committee to the Seventh Meeting of the Parties,* 25 November 1995 (UNEP/OzL.Pro.7/7).

[25] Montreal Protocol, Article 10A(b).

the threshold. In 1994 the parties decided that such countries would not be requested to contribute to the Fund but were equally urged not to request financial assistance from it, as for the most part they were the richer and more dynamic developing countries, such as the Republic of Korea. Such countries could still, however, seek support in the form of technology transfer.[26]

The question of phase-out schedules for Article 5 countries has thus become very closely intertwined with the issues of financial and technology support. Article 5.8 of the Protocol required a review, not later than 1995, of 'the situation of the Parties operating under paragraph 1 of this Article, including the effective implementation of financial cooperation and transfer of technology to them'; in the light of this review, control schedules were to be drawn up for ODS phase-out. The Vienna Meeting in 1995 duly considered a range of phase-out scenarios for Annex A and B substances following the ten-year grace period, and also for Annex C and E substances (HCFCs, HBFCs and methyl bromide). Table 2.2 sets out the control measures that were agreed. Developing countries took the opportunity, both at Vienna and at the preceding meetings of the Open-Ended Working Group, to stress repeatedly that their ability to phase out ODS depended on adequate support, refusing at one point even to discuss hypothetical possibilities for phase-out dates until agreement had been reached on enhanced financial support and technology transfer. The Vienna Meeting finally agreed in principle that the next three-year replenishment of the Multilateral Fund, due for discussion in 1996, should reflect the additional incremental costs of new control measures,[27] though some countries, including France and the US (whose Environmental Protection Agency is currently suffering severe budget cuts), were clearly unhappy at the prospect of higher contributions.

The operation of the Multilateral Fund was in any case subject to a thorough review during 1995. Up to late 1995, a total of $420 million had been allocated to eliminate a projected 63,000 ozone-depleting potential

---

[26] Decision VI/5 of the Parties to the Montreal Protocol, para. (e).

[27] 'To stress that the adoption of any new control measures . . . will require additional funding which will need to be reflected in the replenishment of the Multilateral Fund in 1996 and beyond and in the implementation of technology transfer': Decision VII/4 of the Parties to the Montreal Protocol, para. 2.

Table 2.2: Evolving control measures of the Montreal Protocol: Article 5 countries (%)[a]

Annex A, Group I: CFCs (CFC-11, 12, 113, 114, 115) (reference year 1995–7 average, or 0.3 kg per capita (total for Annex A ODS), whichever is lower)

2002	2005	2007	2010
100	50	15	0

Annex A, Group II: Halons (1211, 1301, 2402) (reference year 1995–7 average, or 0.3 kg per capita (total for Annex A ODS), whichever is lower)

2002	2005	2010
100	50	0

Annex B, Group I: Other fully halogenated CFCs (10 substances) (reference year 1998–2000 average, or 0.2 kg per capita (total for Annex B ODS), whichever is lower)

2003	2007	2010
80	15	0

Annex B, Group II: Carbon tetrachloride (reference year 1998–2000 average, or 0.2 kg per capita (total for Annex B ODS), whichever is lower)

2005	2010
15	0

Annex B, Group III: Methyl chloroform (reference year 1998–2000 average, or 0.2 kg per capita (total for Annex B ODS), whichever is lower)

2003	2005	2010	2015
100	70	30	0

Annex C, Group I: HCFCs (40 substances) (reference year 2015)[b]

2016	2040
100	0

Annex C, Group II: HBFCs (34 substances)

1996
0

Annex E: Methyl bromide (reference year 1995–8 average)[c]

2002
100

[a] Figures shown are consumption and production levels permitted by 1 January of the indicated year, compared to consumption and production levels in the reference year. (The reference years for baseline data, agreed in Decision VII/9 of the Parties, still have to be formally incorporated into the text of the Protocol.)

[b] The controls apply only to the consumption of HCFCs, as for non-Article 5 countries. The 1995 Meeting of the Parties agreed to consider the need for further adjustments to this phase-out schedule by the year 2000.

[c] This excludes use for quarantine and pre-shipment applications.

(ODP)-weighted tonnes of ODS, though only 7,500 tonnes had actually been phased out;[28] another 25,000 and 19,000 ODP-tonnes, respectively, are expected to be added by the end of 1996.[29] Although projects are now being completed more rapidly, this has been regarded as something of a disappointing record, and helps to explain why donor countries have not always been enthusiastic about substantial increases in the Fund's financing. However, late payment from a number of donors resulted in December 1994 in the first instance of a shortfall (of $9.4 million), and the likely inability of many east European and former Soviet states to meet their funding commitments means that the full $510 million is unlikely to be collected. Although it is claimed by many developing countries that the amounts pledged so far are insufficient to cover the full incremental costs of developing country phase-outs, donors believe that they are sufficient, at least to meet the current phase-out schedules. The Fund's Executive Committee has estimated that a total of just over $3 billion will be needed for full phase-out of Annex A and B ODS by 2010, implying an annual rate of disbursement of just under $200 million.[30]

The Fund has of course been subject to many, sometimes conflicting, pressures. 'Because of the Fund's much-praised openness,' commented a recent review, 'it has come under pressure to do many potentially incompatible things: to phase out ozone-depleting substances efficiently, quickly, and cost-effectively; to support projects in most or all of the Article 5 countries; to promote emerging, environmentally-friendly technology; and to avoid subsidising the operations of multinational corporations or production directed to export.'[31] This variety of goals may be hampering the most efficient phase-out schedule, in spreading resources thinly across many countries. A further problem has arisen over whether recipients have an obligation to limit consumption other than via Fund-supported projects; some countries, for example, have sought financial support for converting

---

[28] *OzonAction* 17, January 1996, p. 8.
[29] *Report of the Executive Committee on the Financial Planning in the Multilateral Fund,* 23 November 1995 (UNEP/OzL.Pro.7/8), p. 9.
[30] Ibid., pp. 7–8.
[31] Edward A. Parson and Owen Greene, 'The complex chemistry of the international ozone agreements', *Environment* 37:2, March 1995, p. 39.

one CFC plant while at the same time constructing or purchasing another new one. Lack of financial support is then cited as the reason for not converting the whole sector. The 1995 review concentrated on developing a more systematic approach to policy development, project evaluation and monitoring, and on greater coordination between implementing agencies; a framework for a three-year rolling business plan was approved and should be introduced from 1996. Nevertheless, the Fund has proved its importance to the Montreal Protocol, not only in terms of funding phase-out, but also by boosting membership and participation among developing countries.

2.5 Institutions and procedures

The international institutions established by the Montreal Protocol are set out in Figure 2.1. The main decision-making body is the Meeting of the Parties, which can amend the Protocol's text and adjust its control schedules. Meeting annually, it must review the control measures on the basis of available scientific, environmental, technical and economic information at least every four years, and in fact has done so more frequently (London, 1990; Copenhagen, 1992; Vienna, 1995). Votes require a two-thirds majority, with separate simple majorities of Article 5 and non-Article 5 countries; however, in practice decisions have almost always been taken by consensus. The Open-Ended Working Group of the Parties meets between full sessions to develop and negotiate recommendations for the full Meeting of the Parties.

The Implementation Committee, established in 1990, consists of ten parties (two from each of the five UN regional groups: Africa, Asia-Pacific, Eastern Europe, Latin America and Caribbean, Western Europe and others) and is responsible for reporting to the full Meeting any cases of non-compliance. A non-compliance procedure was finally decided in 1992. A party believed to be failing to meet the control schedules can be dealt with in one of three ways. It may be reported to the Ozone Secretariat by another party, in which case the Secretariat gives the offending country a chance to respond and forwards all documents to the Implementation Committee. Alternatively, the Secretariat can report such

Figure 2.1: International institutions stemming from the Montreal Protocol

OZONE SECRETARIAT

- Located at the United Nations Environment Programme (UNEP) in Nairobi
- Supports both the Vienna Convention and the Montreal Protocol
- Has a staff of eleven including four professionals
- Has an annual budget of $3 million, provided by the parties.

MEETING OF THE PARTIES

- The supreme decision-making body of the Protocol
- Meets annually; can amend the Protocol or adopt related decisions
- Reviews major obligations at least every four years

EXPERT ADVISORY BODIES

Protocol Assessment Panels

- Separate panels for science, environmental impact and technology and economics
- Include numerous international experts serving in individual capacities

Ad hoc specialized advisory bodies:

- Created by the parties as needed to advise on specific questions
- Examples include bodies on data reporting and technologies for destroying ozone-depleting substances

OPEN-ENDED WORKING GROUP

- A less formal negotiation group open to all parties
- Meets as necessary, typically two to three times per year
- Does preliminary work for meetings of the parties

EXECUTIVE COMMITTEE OF THE MULTILATERAL FUND

- Governs the Multilateral Fund
- Has seven members each from developing and industrial countries
- Meets three or four times per year
- Uses a double-majority voting system [a]

IMPLEMENTATION COMMITTEE

- Established by the 1990 Meeting of the Parties
- Has ten members selected from the parties
- Meets once or twice per year
- Considers questions of implementation and non-compliance

FUND SECRETARIAT

- Supports the Executive Committee in managing the fund
- Effectively under UNEP, but located in Montreal
- Has a staff of 15, including eight professionals

IMPLEMENTING AGENCIES

- World Bank, United Nations Development Programme (UNDP), United Nations Environment Programme (UNEP), and United Nations Industrial Development Organization (UNIDO)
- Develop and implement phase-out plans and projects

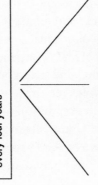

[a] Decisions require an overall majority of two-thirds, with a majority of both developing and industrial countries in favour

Source: Adapted from Edward A. Parson and Owen Greene, 'The complex chemistry of the international ozone agreements', *Environment* 37:2, March 1995.

a country to the Committee directly; or the offending party can report itself. The Implementation Committee is then responsible for recommending appropriate action to the next Meeting of the Parties; this can include provision of technical or financial assistance, the issuing of cautions, or suspension of the party from the Protocol (which would open it to the trade sanctions described in Chapter 3, as well as cutting it off from financial support and institutional arrangements). The procedure is carefully designed to allow maximum opportunity for amicable settlement; the 1995 Meeting in Vienna was the first occasion of its use, and indicated the potential weakness of its 'soft' approach (see Chapter 6).

Expert advisory bodies are established as necessary within the Protocol's structures; they currently comprise the Scientific Assessment Panel (responsible for reviewing scientific knowledge on ozone depletion), the Environmental Effects Assessment Panel (surveying information on the impact of ozone depletion and UV-B irradiation), and the Technology and Economic Assessment Panel (analysing technical options for and economic costs of controlling the use of ODS, including reviewing applications for essential use exemptions). The Ozone Secretariat, part of UNEP and based in Nairobi, provides all the necessary secretarial support for both the Montreal Protocol and the Vienna Convention. Parties to the Protocol agree to provide the Secretariat with data on production and consumption levels of ODS and to share technical information.

The Multilateral Fund is organized slightly separately, largely because if it had fallen under UNEP's wing when founded, it would have been subject to the standard UN administrative support charge. The Fund Secretariat is accordingly based in Montreal, although for most purposes it functions as part of UNEP. It is governed by a separate Executive Committee, however, which consists of representatives of seven Article 5 and seven non-Article 5 countries; it meets three or four times a year and uses the same voting system as the Meeting of the Parties. The Committee is responsible for developing and monitoring the implementation of operational policies, guidelines and administrative arrangements, including the disbursement of resources.

2.6 The impact of the ozone regime

The Montreal Protocol is widely regarded as one of the most effective international environmental treaties in existence. It has proved to be a flexible but robust regime, capable of evolving over time in response to new developments in science and technology; 'an inspiring example of foresight in international management and constructive cooperation between government, industry and science'.[32] In the mid-1980s the international debate was characterized by considerable doubt over the extent and causes of ozone depletion and the feasibility of ameliorative action. Just ten years later, the Meeting of the Parties in Vienna in December 1995, marking the tenth anniversary of the original Vienna Convention, was able to agree the third major set of revisions to the control schedules agreed in 1987. CFCs, whose production levels under the original agreement were still to have been 80% of 1986 levels, should now have been phased out completely in industrialized countries. Production of halons, which was simply to have been capped under the original agreement, ceased at the end of 1993 in non-Article 5 countries. Other chemicals not even thought of as ozone-depleting substances a decade ago have been brought under the coverage of the agreements and their own control schedules progressively tightened.

The record of the ozone regime

By October 1995, a total of 151 countries had ratified the 1985 Vienna Convention and 150 the 1987 Montreal Protocol; 103 had ratified the 1990 London Amendment and 48 the 1992 Copenhagen Amendment.[33] Production and consumption figures for the various controlled substances have changed quite dramatically (see Figure 2.2 and Table 2.3). By the end of 1993 production and consumption of the original controlled CFCs and halons (Annex A substances) had fallen by between 66% and 74% in non-Article 5 countries, seeming well on schedule for phase-out by the end of 1995.[34] In September 1995, DuPont, the original producer of CFCs,

---

[32] Ibid., p. 16.

[33] *OzonAction* 17, January 1996, p. 10.

[34] The end of 1993 is the latest date for which figures are available. These figures relate only to parties reporting data to the Ozone Secretariat, and therefore do not include most of the former Soviet states, among which Russia is a sizeable producer.

Figure 2.2: World-wide production of ozone-depleting substances, 1940–93

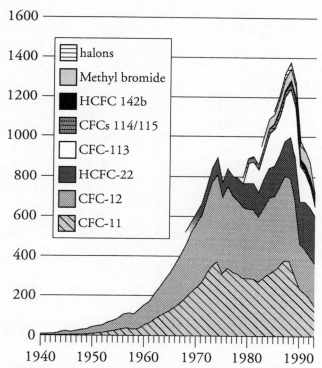

Sources: Methyl bromide data: Methyl Bromide Global Coalition; other ODS: Alternative Fluorocarbon Environmental Acceptability Study, based on independent survey of 19 companies excluding China, India and the CIS. Reproduced from 'Vienna plus ten', *OzonAction* special supplement, November 1995, by kind permission of UNEP Industry and Environment OzonAction Programme.

announced the closure of its Montague plant in Michigan; this was the last DuPont plant producing CFC-11 and CFC-12 anywhere in the developed world.[35] Although both production and consumption had increased in Article 5 countries, production figures there were still only about a quarter

[35] *Global Environmental Change Report* VII:19, 6 October 1995, p. 7. The plant could probably have shut down earlier, but the US government asked DuPont to continue producing CFCs in 1995 to ensure adequate supplies for servicing existing air-conditioners and refrigerators after phase-out in 1996: *Global Environmental Change Report* V:24, 23 December 1993, p. 1.

Table 2.3: Production and consumption data for ozone-depleting substances, 1993

	Production			Consumption		
	1993	Base	% change	1993	Base	% change
(a) Non-Article 5 parties						
AI	302,248.5	921,727.0	-67	136,353.5	528,761.3	-74
AII	53,227.0	158,368.0	-66	30,872.6	104,250.2	-70
BI	960.0	3,017.0	-68	3,409.6	2,927.5	16
BII	-374,076.8	203,564.9	-284	-123,434.2	111,371.0	-211
BIII	27,951.4	69,160.5	-60	17,196.4	46,240.5	-63
CI	8,719.8	7,706.6	13	5,348.2	2,649.1	102
CII	0.0	—	—	0.0	—	—
E	-94.6	-32.1	195	1,686.7	1,482.5	14
(b) Article 5 parties						
AI	82,960.0	44,337.8	87	133,532.3	92,967.6	44
AII	15,412.0	11,200.0	38	19,211.9	24,200.1	-21
BI	0.0	—	—	257.2	91.7	180
BII	-25,412.0	64,040.5	-140	68,137.4	68,669.8	-1
BIII	85.3	1,157.2	-93	3,791.5	4,127.1	-8
CI	1,491.2	731.8	104	2,373.7	1,275.1	86
CII	0.0	—	—	0.0	—	—
E	3.1	86.8	-96	1,062.5	1,265.1	-16
(c) All parties						
AI	385,208.5	966,064.8	-60	269,885.8	621,728.9	-57
AII	68,639.0	169,568.0	-60	50,084.6	128,450.2	-61
BI	960.0	3,017.0	-68	3,666.7	3,019.2	21
BII	-399,488.8	267,605.4	-249	-55,296.8	180,040.9	-131
BIII	28,036.7	70,317.7	-60	20,987.9	50,367.6	-58
CI	10,211.0	8,438.4	21	7,721.9	3,924.2	97
CII	0.0	—	—	0.0	—	—
E	-91.5	54.7	-267	2,749.1	2,747.6	0

Units: ODP-weighted tonnes. (Negative figures refer to use as feedstock.)
Source: Report of the Secretariat on Information Provided by the Parties in Accordance with Articles 4, 7 and 9 of the Montreal Protocol and the Report of the Implementation Committee, 25 September 1995 (UNEP/OzL.Pro.7/6).

of those of non-Article 5 countries, giving a decline in overall world production of about 60% from the base year, 1986.

This outcome is evident in the atmospheric growth rates of the major ozone-depleting chemicals, and in particular of the original CFCs and halons, which have observably slowed.[36] The atmospheric concentration of carbon tetrachloride (controlled after the 1990 London Meeting) has actually decreased. Total organic chlorine (the best overall measure of the potential for ozone depletion) in the troposphere increased by 60 parts per trillion (ppt) per year (1.6%) in 1992, compared to 110 ppt/year in 1989. Peak total chlorine and bromine loading in the troposphere may already have occurred (in 1994–5) and levels now appear to be falling (see Figure 2.3). Stratospheric levels lag by about three to five years, giving a peak rate of global ozone depletion in about 1998–2000. Compared to the late 1960s, maximum ozone losses are predicted to be 12–13% at northern mid-latitudes in winter and spring, and 6–7% in summer and autumn, with about 11% losses in southern mid-latitudes round the year. Further volcanic eruptions or particularly cold Arctic winters could lead to greater losses in particular years. If the Montreal Protocol control regimes for ODS are fully implemented, global ozone levels should gradually recover after 2000, with the Antarctic ozone hole finally closing around the middle of the next century.

As would be expected, the atmospheric abundance of several of the CFC substitutes is observably increasing. Tropospheric chlorine in the form of HCFCs increased in 1992 by about 10 ppt (about 15% of total tropospheric chlorine growth), compared to 5 ppt in 1989 (5% of total growth)[37] – this was of course before any controls on HCFC consumption came into force. Table 2.3 shows the rise in production and consumption figures for HCFCs (CI); the numbers, in ODP-tonnes, are much smaller than those for CFCs because of HCFCs' much smaller ODP. Manufacturers are already, however, beginning to move out of HCFC production into hydrofluorocarbons (HFCs) which, since they do not contain chlorine, do not deplete the ozone layer at all (though they do possess quite high global warming potentials). Atmospheric concentrations of

---

[36] UNEP, *Scientific Assessment of Ozone Depletion: 1994.*
[37] Ibid.

Figure 2.3: Atmospheric chlorine loading, 1960–2080

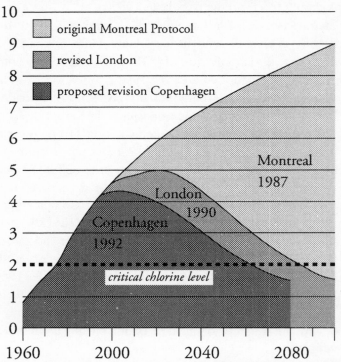

Source: World Meteorological Organization; reproduced from 'Vienna plus ten', *OzonAction* special supplement, November 1995, by kind permission of UNEP Industry and Environment OzonAction Programme.

HFC-134a are currently rising by about 100% a year, from a level so low as to be undetectable prior to 1989, to 0.44 ppt in early 1994 and 1.73 ppt in mid-1995.[38]

Alternatives to ozone-depleting substances: Annexes A and B

In general, CFC consumers in industrialized countries have found it much easier to end their use of CFCs than was originally anticipated – demonstrating the stimulus to innovation provided by a clear regulatory

[38] *Geophysical Research Letters* 23, 15 January 1996, pp. 169–72.

Box 2.2: Major alternative substances and technologies

Use	Alternatives
Aerosols	Finger or trigger pumps, mechanical dispensers, non-fluorocarbon propellants (hydrocarbons, carbon dioxide, compressed air, etc.)
Refrigeration	Domestic: hydrocarbons, HFCs; commercial: hydrocarbons, HCFCs, HFCs, ammonia; mobile air-conditioning: HFCs
Solvents	'No clean' processes, aqueous solutions, hydrocarbons, HCFCs
Foams	Carbon dioxide, hydrocarbons, water, HCFCs
Firefighting	HFCs, water mist or sprinklers, carbon dioxide, dry powder

---

environment such as the Montreal Protocol regime. Major alternatives are described in Box 2.2.

In general, industry has overestimated the demand for fluorocarbon alternatives to CFCs, and is experiencing much slower than expected returns on investments in HCFCs and HFCs. In 1989 DuPont estimated that by the year 2000 global CFC consumption could be replaced by a mixture of HCFCs (30%), HFCs (9%), conservation and reuse (25%) and 'not-in-kind' alternatives (32%). Four years later the company was estimating replacement proportions of 11% for HCFCs, 15% for HFCs, 29% for conservation and 49% for not-in-kind technologies.[39] One ICI estimate showed a likely global market for HFCs and HCFCs of about 200,000 tonnes a year early next century, compared to about 1 million tonnes a year of CFCs in the mid-1980s.[40]

Not-in-kind – i.e. non-fluorocarbon – substitutes have been particularly important in the electronics sector, where a high-technology industry used to rapid innovation has developed a wide range of alternatives, such as 'no-clean' techniques and water-soluble chemistry, but also in the aerosols and foam sectors. Often the substitutes have been found to be both less

---

[39] *Global Environmental Change Report* V:12, 24 June 1993.
[40] Geoffrey Tudhope, Managing Director ICI Fluorochemicals, quoted in *Financial Times,* survey of the chemicals industry, 27 October 1995, p. 4.

costly and more effective than the fluorocarbon-based techniques they replaced.[41] A small but dramatic illustration is provided by the Royal Canadian Mint's decision, in autumn 1995, to convert its coin blank cleaning operations from a CFC-based vapour degreasing process to an ultrasonic aqueous system. The cost of the solution now used is approximately C$1,000–1,500 a year, compared to 1994 expenses of C$200,000 for CFCs; the payback period for the new equipment was less than one year.[42] Refrigeration and air-conditioning is the sector which has experienced the greatest difficulty in phasing out CFCs, particularly in servicing and retrofitting existing units (which have lifetimes as long as 25 years), where HCFC blends have so far proved the only feasible alternatives. New equipment, however, is increasingly using HFCs, ammonia (the chemical used in the very first refrigerators early in the century) or hydrocarbons, as in, for example, the 'greenfreeze' domestic refrigerator promoted by Greenpeace.

Phase-out of CFCs in the EU was achieved a year earlier than the Montreal Protocol deadline (1 January 1995), but was only managed in this sector by recycling and extensive stockpiling by users; it is not yet clear whether the sector will experience serious difficulty as stockpiles run out. Illegal imports of CFCs almost certainly also contributed (see further in Chapter 6). Stockpiling, or 'banking', has also been important in the phase-out of halon production, which was achieved in developed countries (apart from Russia and a number of other economies in transition: see Chapter 6) by 1 January 1994. Effective banking strategies are expected to provide adequate supplies until the early years of the next century, an important achievement since alternatives do not yet exist for all the fire-fighting applications of halons.

Annex B substances – a range of fully halogenated CFCs which it is technically possible to manufacture but which have never been produced in significant quantities, plus carbon tetrachloride and methyl chloroform

---

[41] There have been some concerns over the safety of hydrocarbon-based alternatives, however; at one stage a proposal was made for an essential use exemption for the use of CFCs in aerosol cans of 'silly string', much used at children's birthday parties – which tend to feature lit candles.

[42] *Global Environmental Change Report* VII:23, 8 December 1995, p. 8.

– were all phased out at the end of 1995 in non-Article 5 countries (though significant production of carbon tetrachloride continues for feedstock). Problems are not expected with phase-out of these ODS; as noted above, the tropospheric abundance of carbon tetrachloride, which was mainly used in the production of CFC-11 and -12, has already fallen. Methyl chloroform is a solvent, and has largely been replaced through the use of other chlorinated solvents and hydrocarbons.

Eight developing countries (Argentina, Brazil, China, India, Republic of Korea, Mexico, Romania and Venezuela) currently produce ODS, mostly through directly owned subsidiaries of transnational corporations.[43] Article 5 countries are not as yet subject to any controls on ODS; the ten-year grace period for Annex A and B substances is not due to come to an end until 1999, and total phase-out is not required until 2010. In fact, however, many of them have already made substantial progress in reducing their use of CFCs, halons, methyl chloroform and carbon tetrachloride. As the 1994 report of UNEP's Technology and Economic Assessment Panel (TEAP) commented, 'industrial innovation has occurred more rapidly than anticipated and there has been much more rapid progress than predicted in commercialising replacements, including non-HCFC, for CFCs and halons.'[44] Phase-out has been encouraged particularly in exporting countries by importers' unwillingness to purchase products containing ODS which are soon to be phased out (see Chapter 5). China, for example, aims to phase out Annex A and B substances by 2005, and India has announced that it expects to improve on the 2010 deadline (the exact timing, however, depends on the size of the funding available under the Multilateral Fund).[45]

---

[43] Out of total Article 5 production of CFCs (Annex A, Group I) in 1993, China produced about 40% and Brazil, India and Mexico about 15% each. These figures exclude Taiwan, which is a CFC producer but, as a non-signatory of the Protocol, does not formally report data. UNEP, *Report of the Secretariat to the Seventh Meeting of the Parties to the Montreal Protocol,* 25 September 1995 (UNEP/OzL.Pro.7/6).

[44] *1994 Report of the Technology and Economic Assessment Panel; 1995 Assessment* (Nairobi: UNEP, 1994), p. 57.

[45] *OzonAction* 17, January 1996, p. 10.

Alternatives to ozone-depleting substances: Annexes C and E

Phase-out efforts in non-Article 5 countries are now being concentrated on HCFCs (Annex C, Group I) and methyl bromide (Annex E).

Parties to the Montreal Protocol are enjoined to ensure that HCFCs are used only as direct replacements for other ODS where other more environmentally suitable alternatives are not available.[46] HCFCs were critical in meeting the early CFC phase-out goals, but are generally considered much less important for new equipment available in the medium and long term; technically (though not yet always economically) viable alternatives exist for almost all current uses. The EU agreed in 1994 to implement a complete phase-out by 2015, 15 years ahead of the Copenhagen phase-out date of 2030. [47] The US, however, where industry had moved out of CFCs earlier through investing more heavily in HCFCs, resisted any adjustment of the phase-out dates at the Vienna Meeting in 1995. Compromise was finally reached through a reduction in the figure used for calculating baseline consumption and an agreement that consumption in the last ten years before phase-out would be used only for servicing existing equipment (a 'service tail'). At the close of the meeting, however, a declaration was issued on behalf of 24 countries[48] stating their intention to limit the use of HCFCs as soon as possible and calling for stronger control measures. This was particularly important to Article 5 countries, for which the HCFC phase-out schedule agreed at Vienna was thought by many to be unnecessarily weak, with no controls at all to be applied until 2016, and with a baseline not to be set until 2015, allowing 20 further years of unrestrained consumption.

The phase-out of HCFCs is influenced by the rate of adoption of HFC-based technologies. HFCs, as mentioned above, are not ozone depleters and therefore cannot be controlled under the Montreal Protocol. As they possess significant global warming potentials, however, they are relevant to the continuing negotiations on the Climate Change Convention. It seems entirely possible that, given the difficulties surrounding the control of car-

---

[46] Montreal Protocol, Article 2F, para. 7.

[47] EC Regulation 3093/94 (15 December 1994).

[48] 14 west European, 8 Latin American and 2 African.

bon dioxide emissions, any eventual climate change agreement may attempt to limit the use of HFCs. This in turn will have a knock-on effect on further developments of the Montreal Protocol, acting as a disincentive for manufacturers to switch out of HCFCs into HFCs – though it would also increase the attractiveness of not-in-kind alternatives. Governments in many industrialized countries are currently attempting to draw up voluntary agreements with industry to limit HFC use; in January 1996, the UK announced its first such agreements, covering the aerosol, air-conditioning and refrigeration, fire protection and foam industries, aiming to limit both use and emissions of HFCs.[49] If these prove ineffective, regulation may be necessary.

The application of controls to the production and consumption of methyl bromide (Annex E of the Montreal Protocol) has proved a more contentious issue. This is partly because it concerns a largely different set of producers and consumers from those involved in fluorocarbons, and also because alternatives are less easily available. Major sources of methyl bromide in the atmosphere include the ocean, which is a natural source, accounting for more than half of the total, plus three anthropogenic sources: agricultural use (primarily fumigation, to control pests and weeds; such treatment is often required by importers), biomass burning and car exhausts.[50] This last use was probably dominant in methyl bromide emissions until the 1970s; since then, however, bromine use in fuel additives has declined rapidly.

Attention has therefore focused on agricultural uses, where UNEP's Methyl Bromide Technical Options Committee estimated that technically feasible alternatives were available, or at an advanced state of development, for up to 90% of all methyl bromide uses in non-Article 5 countries – though opinions diverged widely on the possible speed and costs of phase-out.[51] The chemical has been increasingly subject to controls in industrialized countries in any case because of concerns about toxicity; the Netherlands, for example, has already virtually eliminated its use. After much internal debate, the EU as a whole adopted a target of a 25%

[49] *Global Environmental Change Report* VIII:3, 9 February 1996, p. 7.
[50] UNEP, *Scientific Assessment of Ozone Depletion: 1994.*
[51] UNEP, *1994 Report of the Technology and Economic Assessment Panel,* p. 90.

reduction from 1991 levels by 1998.[52] The provisions of its Clean Air Act mandate the US to phase out completely any ozone-depleting substance with an ODP greater than 0.2 (that of methyl bromide is estimated at 0.6) seven years after its listing by the EPA administrator, regardless of the actual controls applied internationally – which, since it was listed when the Copenhagen Amendment entered into force in 1994, means by 1 January 2001. The US was therefore unsurprisingly keen to see similar controls extended to all Montreal Protocol parties, and a control schedule was agreed at Vienna in 1995 (see Table 2.1), with ultimate phase-out by 2010. Use for quarantine and pre-shipment purposes is exempted from the controls, however, and the possibility remains of a further 'critical agricultural use' exemption (proposed by the US) after total phase-out – though critics charged that this description could potentially be applied to 30–40% of current uses.[53]

A control schedule for methyl bromide was also agreed, for the first time, for Article 5 countries: a freeze in 2002 at the average production and consumption levels of the period 1995–8. A strong developing country lobby, led by Kenya,[54] Morocco and India, argued against the principle of any controls until further studies, financial support and technology transfer had taken place. These countries concentrated on the importance of methyl bromide to food production in Article 5 countries, which currently account for about 18% of total global use in agriculture.[55] The chemical is primarily used for pest and disease control in the production of particular high-value cash crops such as tobacco, cut flowers or vegetables. In contrast to CFCs, there are as yet no easy alternatives to the use of methyl bromide; not-in-kind alternatives such as Integrated Pest Management techniques are difficult to apply in developing countries without substantial further research and training. However, relatively little food production and storage actually depends on the use of the chemical, and many devel-

---

[52] EC Regulation 3093/94 (15 December 1994).

[53] *Global Environmental Change Report* VII:23, 8 December 1995, p. 2, and VIII:4, 23 February 1996, p. 3.

[54] Rumours persisted in linking Kenyan opposition to controls on methyl bromide to plans by the Israeli company Dead Sea Bromide, one of the world's largest producers, to build a production plant in Kenya.

[55] UNEP, *1994 Report of the Technology and Economic Assessment Panel*, p. 93.

oping countries are experimenting with alternatives. A number of Latin American countries publicly disagreed with the hitherto united developing country position at the Vienna Meeting, and three Article 5 countries joined ten non-Article 5 parties in a 'declaration on methyl bromide' similar in intent to that on HCFCs (see above). The controls on methyl bromide agreed at Vienna will in any case be subject to a review and consideration of further adjustments at the 1997 Meeting, following a report to be prepared by the TEAP.[56]

Conclusion

The development of the Montreal Protocol phase-out regimes can by and large be regarded as a success story, at least in most of the industrialized world. The 1995 Vienna Meeting, however, marked the end of the initial phase of the ozone regime, in which effort was concentrated primarily on identifying the various ozone-depleting substances and on agreeing control schedules for them. Attention is now turning increasingly to issues of implementation, including compliance with the agreed controls. Many of these have implications for the trade aspects of the ozone regime, which is the primary subject of this study. Before examining them, however, we turn to an analysis and history of the trade measures of the Montreal Protocol.

---

[56] Decision VII/8 of the Parties to the Montreal Protocol.

Chapter 3

Trade and the Montreal Protocol

The central aim of this report is to analyse the relationship between the international trading system and the Montreal Protocol, as an exemplar of a multilateral environmental agreement. This chapter accordingly describes the trade-related elements of the Protocol and examines their salience in the negotiation of the treaty and the evolution of the regime it has established. The trade aspects of the treaty fall into two categories: trade restrictions between parties, which are not mandated by the Protocol but are consequential on the control schedules; and trade restrictions between parties and non-parties, which are required under the terms of the Protocol.

3.1 Trade restrictions between parties

If parties to the Montreal Protocol are to meet the requirements of the control schedules, they must implement some method of controlling imports of ODS, as these count towards the consumption figure for the country as a whole. A wide variety of restrictions on trade in ODS have followed from the policy regimes adopted by the parties in their efforts to achieve phase-out. The main ones are listed in Box 3.1.

In addition to the various policy instruments adopted, and irrespective of the stage of phase-out, all parties to the Protocol are required to report consumption and production – which must include export and import – data to the Ozone Secretariat. Since most countries are not ODS producers, this requires a monitoring and tracking system organized through customs declarations. Because the international Harmonized Commodity Description and Coding System assigned codes to chemicals according to their function rather than chemical properties, the international Customs Cooperation Council has established a new set of codes for monitoring

---

Box 3.1: Policy instruments for phasing out ozone-depleting substances: impacts on trade

Instrument	*Used in (not exhaustive)*
Voluntary industry agreements to restrict imports	Netherlands, Norway
Product labelling requirements	Czech Republic, Germany, US
Requirement for import licences	Czech Republic, EU, Taiwan, Thailand, US; fee required: Australia, Hong Kong
Permit trading system for import allowances	Hong Kong, Mexico (planned), New Zealand, Singapore, US
Import duty reductions on non-ODS products	Indonesia (planned)
Import duty reductions on non-ODS technologies (e.g. recycling equipment)	Ghana (total exemption), Malaysia, Thailand
Excise taxes on ODS	Chile (planned), China (planned), Czech Republic, Denmark, Taiwan (planned), US; low level, designed to cover administration costs of phase-out: Australia
Quantitative restrictions on imports of ODS or products containing ODS	China, EU
Total or partial bans on imports of ODS	Sweden, US
Total or partial bans on imports of products containing ODS	Finland, Singapore, Sweden
Total or partial bans on imports of ODS-producing technologies	Malaysia

Source: Adapted from *1994 Report of the Economic Options Committee; 1995 Assessment* (Nairobi: UNEP, 1994), pp. 4-4–4-15, and unpublished material.

ODS, with a separate number for each controlled substance. Customs authorities record data using these codes, and transfer the information to the government agency responsible for ODS monitoring and reporting. Complications have arisen with misreporting by importers (especially after

Table 3.1: Comparison of production, import and export of substances, 1993

	Production			Import			Export		
	1993	Base	% change	1993	Base	% change	1993	Base	% change
Article 5 parties									
AI	829,60.0	44,337.7	87	70,945.5	49,831.6	42	20,373.1	1,201.8	1,595
AII	154,12.0	11,200.0	38	4,957.3	13,000.1	-62	1,157.4	0.0	—
BI	0.0	0.0	—	257.2	91.7	180	0.0	0.0	—
BII	-254,12.0	64,040.5	-140	128,570.2	14,276.7	801	35,020.8	9,647.4	263
BIII	85.3	1,157.2	-93	3,718.9	3,017.0	23	12.7	47.1	-73
CI	1,491.2	731.8	104	1,090.0	2,423.2	-55	2,07.5	15.3	1,257
CII	0.0	0.0	—	0.0	0.0	—	0.0	0.0	—
E	3.1	86.8	-96	1,059.4	1,178.3	-10	0.0	0.0	—
TOTAL	74,539.5	121,554.1	-39	210,598.5	83,818.6	151	56,771.6	10,911.7	420
Non-Article 5 parties									
AI	302,248.5	921,727.0	-67	61,886.3	99,534.3	-38	82,392.0	65,135.6	26
AII	53,227.0	158,368.0	-66	8,020.6	38,490.1	-79	5,197.0	19,091.0	-73
BI	960.0	3,017.0	-68	2,565.5	71.5	3487	77.9	77.0	1
BII	-374,076.8	203,564.9	-284	90,197.9	77,551.3	16	49,320.9	98,236.0	-50
BIII	27,951.4	69,160.5	-60	3,169.3	8,825.9	-64	48,96.6	10,323.4	-53
CI	8,719.8	7,706.6	13	1,195.8	5,310.8	-77	1,016.6	667.5	52
CII	0.0	0.0	—	0.0	0.0	—	0.0	0.0	—
E	-94.6	-32.1	195	1,783.4	2,846.0	-37	739.2	80.5	818
TOTAL	18,935.3	1,363,511.9	-99	168,818.9	232,629.9	-27	143,640.4	193,611.0	-26

Units: ODP-weighted tonnes. (Negative figures refer to use as feedstock, though in 1995 the parties decided that ODS exported and imported for feedstock should not be included in the calculations of consumption or production in the exporting country, or in consumption in the importing country, provided that the importer gave a guarantee that use would be solely for feedstock; trade data were still to be provided to the Ozone Secretariat: Decision VII/30 of the Parties to the Montreal Protocol.)

Source: Report of the Secretariat on Information Provided by the Parties in Accordance with Articles 4, 7 and 9 of the Montreal Protocol and the Report of the Implementation Committee, 25 September 1995 (UNEP/OzL.Pro.7/6).

import controls have been established) and misrecording by customs authorities unfamiliar with the substances involved.[57]

The impact on trade of the various control schedules is shown in Table 3.1, which includes import and export data for 1993 compared to base year. As would be expected, non-Article 5 parties have experienced sharp falls in trade in all categories of ODS other than HCFCs and methyl bromide, while Article 5 parties show a more varied picture.

Trade in recycled ozone-depleting substances

As noted in Chapter 2, the parties agreed in 1992 that imports and exports of recycled and used controlled substances should not be included in the calculation of consumption, as long as the relevant data were fully reported to UNEP. This is an important part of the ozone regime, and likely to become more so as production of the various ODS ends; the availability of recycled materials for servicing and maintaining ODS-using equipment, and the potential to trade in recycled and recovered ODS for countries which are phasing out such equipment, will be important factors in minimising adaptation costs.[58] DuPont estimated in 1989 that by the year 2000 25% of pre-Montreal Protocol CFC use would be replaced by conservation and reuse; four years later its estimate had risen to 29% (see Chapter 2). The growing problem of illegal trade in ODS mislabelled or disguised as recycled substances, however, is leading some countries to contemplate restrictions on the movement of recycled chemicals (see Chapter 6). Data for 1993 on the trade in recycled ODS are shown in Table 3.2, though only 35 parties had actually reported any information at all by July 1995.[59]

The Montreal Protocol, however, is not the only multilateral environmental agreement with trade provisions. The Basel Convention on the Control of Transboundary Movements of Hazardous Wastes and their Disposal was negotiated in 1989. It aims to reduce the export and import

---

[57] *1994 Report of the Economic Options Committee; 1995 Assessment* (Nairobi: UNEP, 1994), p. 4-3.

[58] Ibid., p. 6-7.

[59] *Issues for Consideration by the Open-Ended Working Group of the Parties to the Montreal Protocol: Note by the Secretariat*, 5 July 1995 (UNEP/OzL.Pro/WG.12/2/Add.1).

Table 3.2: Import and export of new, used and recycled substances, 1993

	Import			Export		
	New	Used	Recycled	New	Used	Recycled
Article 5 parties						
AI	70,945.5	0.0	0.0	20,373.1	0.0	0.0
AII	4,957.3	0.0	0.0	1,157.4	0.0	0.0
BI	257.2	0.0	0.0	0.0	0.0	0.0
BII	128,570.2	21.8	0.0	35,020.8	0.0	0.0
BIII	3,718.9	0.0	0.0	12.7	0.0	0.0
CI	1,090.0	0.7	0.0	207.5	0.0	0.0
E	1,059.4	0.0	0.0	0.0	0.0	0.0
TOTAL	210,598.5	22.5	0.0	56,771.6	0.0	0.0
Non-Article 5 parties						
AI	61,886.3	780.0	5.8	82,392.0	13.0	0.0
AII	8,020.6	15.0	0.0	5,197.0	10.0	0.0
BI	2,565.5	5.3	0.0	77.9	0.0	0.0
BII	90,197.9	9.0	0.0	49,320.9	0.0	0.0
B III	3,169.3	10.9	0.0	4,896.6	1,602.0	0.0
C I	1,195.8	15.5	0.0	1,016.6	0.0	0.0
E	1,783.4	0.0	0.0	739.2	0.0	0.0
TOTAL	168,818.9	835.7	5.8	143,640.4	1,625.0	0.0

Units: ODP-weighted tonnes.
Source: *Report of the Secretariat on Information Provided by the Parties in Accordance with Articles 4, 7 and 9 of the Montreal Protocol and the Report of the Implementation Committee*, 25 September 1995 (UNEP/OzL.Pro.7/6).

of hazardous wastes, minimize the total amount of them and assist developing countries in their environmentally sound management. It applies to ODS in wastes: halogenated organic solvents are listed in Annex I ('categories of wastes to be controlled') and ecotoxicity is listed in Annex III ('list of hazardous characteristics'). Exemptions, however, are allowed for the export of substances where it can be shown that a superior disposal or recycling technology exists in the importing country.

The Basel Convention therefore affects the shipment of ODS which are being recovered from products containing them and are destined for recycling or safe disposal. In principle, the Convention should permit such trade, but the wording is vague and the parties to the Montreal Protocol recognized in 1993 that it could usefully be clarified.[60] Following discussions between the Ozone and Basel Convention Secretariats, agreement was reached during 1995. Recycled CFCs and halons meeting usable purity specifications prescribed by appropriate organizations, such as the International Standards Organization (ISO), would not be considered to be wastes under the Basel terms. Trade in CFCs and halons which could not meet the purity specifications would then occur under the normal Basel terms, i.e. only if the importing country possessed recycling facilities which could process the imported ODS to those standards.[61]

3.2 Trade restrictions between parties and non-parties

Article 4 of the Montreal Protocol sets out the restrictions parties are required to implement on both imports from and exports to non-parties of three categories: ODS themselves, products containing ODS (e.g. refrigerators) and products made with but not containing ODS (e.g. electronic components). The restrictions applied are different in each case, and are summarized in Table 3.3. The term 'non-party' relates to each successive amendment to the Protocol; for the purpose of trade controls on methyl bromide, for example, a non-party would be a country which had not ratified the Copenhagen Amendment (the first point at which Annex E was introduced), *not* simply one which had not acceded to the Protocol at all.

Restrictions on ozone-depleting substances

The import of Annex A substances (the main CFCs and halons) from non-parties was banned from 1990, one year after the treaty's entry into force. Similarly, Annex B imports (carbon tetrachloride, methyl chloroform and other CFCs) were banned from August 1993, one year after the London Amendment came into effect, and Annex C, Group II imports (HBFCs) were banned from June 1995, one year after the Copenhagen Amendment came into effect.

---

[60] Decision V/24 of the Parties to the Montreal Protocol.
[61] Decision VII/31 of the Parties to the Montreal Protocol.

Table 3.3: Trade restrictions between parties and non-parties

Nature of trade	ODS Annex		
	A	B	C II
Imports of ODS	January 1990	August 1993	June 1995
Exports of ODS	January 1993	August 1993	June 1995
Imports of goods containing ODS			
Listing	January 1992	(August 1995)	June 1997
Ban	January 1993	(August 1996)	June 1998
Imports of goods made with but not containing ODS			
'Determination of			
feasibility'	January 1994	August 1997	June 1999

Notes
Dates set by Montreal Protocol, as amended and adjusted by London and Copenhagen
Meetings. Dates in parentheses relate to restrictions which were not implemented; see text.
The extension of the trade measures to Annex C Group I ODS (HCFCs) was due to be
discussed at the 1995 Vienna Meeting but was not. The extension of the trade measures
to Annex E ODS (methyl bromide) (other than restrictions on goods made with but not
containing methyl bromide) is scheduled to be discussed at the 1996 Costa Rica Meeting.

Exports to non-parties were initially subject to an outright ban only for
exports from Article 5 countries; the ban came into force on 1 January
1993. Other parties were permitted to export to non-parties but from 1993
the quantities involved were to count as part of the exporting country's
consumption, and were thus subject to the normal phase-out schedules. As
developing countries increasingly acceded to the Protocol, however, this
differential treatment became harder to justify. The London and
Copenhagen Amendments accordingly overrode this provision and adopted outright export bans for all countries – for Annex A ODS from January
1993, for Annex B from August 1993 and for Annex C, Group II from June
1995.

Under Article 4, para. 10 of the Montreal Protocol, the parties were
scheduled to consider the extension of the import and export bans to the
remaining ODS (Annex C, Group I – HCFCs – and Annex E – methyl bromide). The Open-Ended Working Group meeting in May 1995, however,

accepted the conclusions of the 1994 TEAP report, which had pointed out the undesirability of restrictions in trade in HCFCs.[62] Not only were these ODS merely transitional substances, but also only a relatively small number of parties had at that time ratified the Copenhagen Amendment and thereby applied any controls at all to them; restrictions on trade could conceivably, therefore, simply encourage extended reliance on CFCs among non-parties to the Copenhagen Amendment. No new trade restrictions on HCFCs, therefore, were introduced. Trade restrictions on methyl bromide would not suffer from the same problems, but the parties still believed it desirable to delay their introduction until more countries had signed the Copenhagen Amendment; the Vienna Meeting therefore decided to consider restrictions on methyl bromide the following year.[63]

Restrictions on products containing ozone-depleting substances

The original Protocol mandated the parties to draw up a list of products containing controlled substances within three years of the agreement entering into force. Parties which did not object to the list would then ban within one year imports of any such products from non-parties. This provision was amended at London and Copenhagen to establish a sequence of ODS-related bans similar to that described above: imports of products containing Annex A ODS were listed from 1 January 1992, and banned from January 1993; imports of products containing Annex B ODS were to be listed from August 1995, and banned from August 1996; and imports of products containing Annex C, Group II ODS are to be listed from June 1997, and banned from June 1998. The Vienna Meeting was to discuss the extension of this process to products containing HCFCs and methyl bromide, but, as above, did not. The 1996 Meeting is now scheduled to discuss import bans for products containing methyl bromide, and the TEAP has been instructed to identify such goods – though there probably are none.[64]

---

[62] UNEP, *1994 Report of the Technology and Economic Assessment Panel*, p. 49.

[63] Decision VII/7 of the Parties to the Montreal Protocol.

[64] Ibid., para. 3; UNEP, *1994 Report of the Technology and Economic Assessment Panel*, p. 51.

The third Meeting of the Parties, in Nairobi in June 1991, duly adopted a list of products containing Annex A ODS, CFCs and halons. This came into force on 27 May 1992 as Annex D of the Protocol, listing six categories of products: automobile and truck air-conditioning units; domestic and commercial refrigeration and air-conditioning/heat pump equipment; aerosol products (except medical aerosols); portable fire extinguishers; insulation boards, panels and pipe covers; and pre-polymers. Personal effects belonging to non-commercial travellers are exempt. As noted above, imports of such products are banned only where parties do not object to their listing; Singapore originally objected to the listing of several, but had withdrawn its objection by 1992.[65] The 1994 Meeting of the Parties should have adopted a listing of products containing Annex B ODS, but after extensive debate decided that it was unnecessary. By that stage, carbon tetrachloride and methyl chloroform were themselves due to be phased out by 1 January 1996, seven months before the product ban would have come into effect, and all significant producers of these substances had ratified the Protocol. 'The work entailed in drawing up and adopting such a list,' concluded the Meeting, 'would be disproportionate to the benefits, if any, to the ozone layer.'[66] It is highly likely that a similar conclusion will be reached during 1996 for products containing Annex C, Group II ODS (HBFCs), since these substances were never in widespread use and already appear to have been phased out.

Exports of products containing ODS are not controlled by the Protocol, as the original negotiators felt that there was little to be gained from such a measure. ODS contained in such products are effectively controlled through the normal phase-out schedules.

Restrictions on products made with but not containing ozone-depleting substances

The final category of trade restrictions in the Protocol applies to products made with, but not actually containing, ODS. When the agreement was originally reached in Montreal, this represented a potentially huge

---

[65] See Decision IV/16 of the Parties to the Montreal Protocol.
[66] Decision VI/12 of the Parties to the Montreal Protocol, para. 2.

number and variety of goods, including anything treated with CFC-containing cleaning and degreasing agents (a wide range, varying from electronics components to metal parts), flash-frozen food or dry-cleaned textiles. The parties thus agreed simply to 'determine the feasibility' of applying trade restrictions to such products within five years of the Protocol's entry into force. [67] As above, this was subsequently amended to create a sequence of 'determinations of feasibility' for the various categories of ODS: Annex A by January 1994, Annex B by August 1997 and Annex C, Group II by June 1999. Deadlines for Annex C, Group I and Annex E were to be decided at the Vienna Meeting but again were not. If controls were determined to be feasible, a procedure was to be followed similar to that for products containing ODS: lists of products were to be drawn up and, in the absence of objections, subject within one year to import bans if originating from non-parties. As above, exports were not to be controlled explicitly, but are effectively restricted through the normal phase-out schedules.

The question of feasibility was discussed at the 1993 Meeting in Bangkok. The TEAP concluded that in at least some cases where ODS had been used in manufacture, trace residues would be present which could be detected through gas chromatography or mass spectrometry – though internationally acceptable procedures and standards would have to be drawn up.[68] In other cases, however, particularly where CFCs had been used as solvents (e.g. in electronic products manufacturing), trace residues were undetectable by these methods and in all probability by any procedure which would be economically feasible. (Detecting even bulk ODS themselves has proved quite difficult for customs authorities: see Chapter 6.)

Furthermore, the range of products which would potentially have to be tested was enormous. If a wide interpretation of 'produced with but not containing' were adopted, covering direct and indirect use, almost every traded product would have to be included, since some stage in its manufacturing process would almost certainly have involved equipment using or made with ODS, even if the product itself was not so treated. The logi-

---

[67] Montreal Protocol, Article 4, para. 4.
[68] See UNEP, *1994 Report of the Economic Options Committee*, pp. 6-5–6-6.

cal conclusion would be to ban all trade with non-parties, a measure not only impossible to implement but also involving costs out of all proportion to the benefits to the ozone layer. Even if a more restrictive definition, involving only direct input of ODS, were adopted, the list of products which would need to be drawn up would be very large – and again, given the very small quantities of ODS involved in the production of each product, the costs in lost trade would vastly exceed the benefits to the ozone layer. The 1994 TEAP report reached similar conclusions with regard to products made with but not containing HCFCs.[69]

Faced with these conclusions, the TEAP recommended that no trade restrictions should be considered. The Bangkok Meeting agreed, while requesting the TEAP to review the issue at regular intervals.[70] The introduction of such controls thus remains a theoretical possibility, and has proved to be of some value in encouraging countries to participate in the Protocol and its amendments: 'There is evidence to suggest that the parties regard it as an important contributor to the effectiveness of the incentive package of the Montreal Protocol.'[71] This is a matter of particular importance for products treated with methyl bromide, since many of these are traded. Trace quantities of methyl bromide do tend to remain in durable and perishable commodities fumigated with the chemical, but usually only for a few days after treatment; elevated bromide ion levels, which are indicative, though not conclusive proof, of treatment, are detectable thereafter. Similarly, crops grown in soil treated with methyl bromide generally show raised bromide content, but natural levels are highly variable between crops and soil types. The 1995 Meeting did *not* refer this matter for consideration in 1996, but at least some parties were prepared to contemplate it (particularly those in competition for markets with non-signatories to Copenhagen, i.e. in this context non-parties), and the methyl bromide industry remains, unsurprisingly, concerned about the future application of such controls.[72]

---

[69] UNEP, *1994 Report of the Technology and Economic Assessment Panel*, p. 50.

[70] Decision V/17 of the Parties to the Montreal Protocol.

[71] Robert van Slooten, 'The case of the Montreal Protocol', in *Trade and Environment: Processes and Production Methods* (Paris: OECD, 1994), p. 89.

[72] Tom Duafala (Methyl Bromide Global Coalition), personal communication.

Other trade provisions

All these restrictions on imports from and exports to non-parties are subject to one general exemption. If a country not party to the Protocol is nevertheless determined by the parties to be in compliance with its control schedules, having submitted data to that effect, it is not subject to any restrictions on trade. In 1992 the parties decided that Colombia, at that time a non-signatory, was in full compliance with the control schedules on the basis of the data it had submitted and would therefore be exempt from trade restrictions.[73] The same Meeting of the Parties also speeded up the process by agreeing that any state which had submitted satisfactory data by the end of March 1993 would be deemed provisionally exempt from the trade provisions; a final decision would be taken by the next Meeting, in November 1993, but the countries concerned would not suffer in the interim.[74] Four countries – Malta, Jordan, Poland and Turkey – duly applied for exemptions pending completion of their procedures for ratifying the London Amendment; exemptions were granted until the 1994 Meeting, provided that adequate data were submitted by the end of March 1994.[75] Malta and Jordan ratified the London Amendment before that date; Poland and Turkey, which had not, subsequently reapplied in 1995 and were again granted exemptions until they had completed ratification, subject to provision of data.[76] Turkey ratified the London Amendment in April 1995 and Poland once again submitted suitable data; in August 1995 the Implementation Committee decided that no further action needed to be taken.[77]

This flexibility in the application of the letter of the Protocol thus enables its aim – the control of ODS – to be satisfied while avoiding legal complexities with countries which are slower in ratifying than in applying its provisions. This provision is also of importance to Taiwan, which is not

---

[73] Decision IV/17B of the Parties to the Montreal Protocol.

[74] Decision IV/17C of the Parties to the Montreal Protocol.

[75] Decision V/3 of the Parties to the Montreal Protocol.

[76] Decision VI/4 of the Parties to the Montreal Protocol.

[77] *Report of the Implementation Committee under the Non-Compliance Procedure for the Montreal Protocol on the Work of its Tenth Meeting*, 30 August 1995 (UNEP/OzL.Pro/ImpCom/10/4), item 4(b).

a signatory due to its lack of international recognition. Since it has adhered to the phase-out schedules, however, it has not been subject to trade restrictions under the Protocol.[78]

In addition to these trade restrictions, Article 4 of the Protocol instructs parties to discourage the export to non-parties of technology for producing and using controlled substances, and to refrain from providing assistance (such as subsidies, export credits or export guarantees) for exports to non-parties of products, equipment or technology. The ODS referred to are the familiar Annex A, B and C Group II list; i.e. excluding HCFCs and methyl bromide. Equipment and technology designed for recovery, recycling and destruction of ODS, or for the promotion of alternatives, is excluded. The Protocol specifies no direct sanctions for breach of these clauses but they are nevertheless commitments, and parties contravening them could arguably be considered to be in non-compliance with the treaty: they are 'soft law'.[79]

3.3 The aims and effectiveness of the trade provisions

Origins of the trade provisions

How important were these trade-restricting provisions in the negotiation of the Montreal Protocol? The topic was first formally raised by the US during the negotiating session in Geneva in December 1986. There were two aims. One was simply to maximize participation in the Protocol, by shutting off non-signatories from supplies of CFCs and halons and providing a significant incentive to join. If completely effective this would in practice render the trade provisions redundant, as there would be no non-parties against which to apply them.

The other goal, should participation not prove total, was to prevent industrial production from migrating to non-signatory countries to escape the phase-out schedules and simply re-exporting ODS to its original hosts. In the absence of trade restrictions, this could fatally undermine the control measures, countering attempts to limit emissions in the signatory

---

[78] Parson and Greene, 'Complex chemistry', p. 36 n. 12.
[79] James A. Losey (formerly US EPA), personal communication.

countries. It could also help non-signatory countries to gain a competitive advantage over signatories, as the progressive phase-outs raised industrial production costs for adherents to the treaty. The development of alternatives to CFCs would be drastically hindered – which helps to explain industry's enthusiasm for the trade provisions. If trade were forbidden, however, non-signatories would not only be unable to export ODS, but would also be unable to enjoy fully the potential gains from cheaper production as exports of products containing, and eventually made with, ODS, would also be restricted. (In fact, as industrial innovation proceeded far more quickly than expected, many of the substitutes proved significantly cheaper than the original ODS – but this could not have been foreseen in 1987.)

Negotiators disagreed in retrospect as to the relative importance of these twin aims. Some believed that maximizing participation was the primary objective, while others felt that this was merely a side-effect of controls chiefly directed at preventing industrial migration.[80] Different individuals and government departments involved in the negotiations probably had different objectives; while environment ministries and agencies, for instance, probably saw participation as the desirable goal, departments of trade and commerce would be likely to be more concerned over industrial migration. In fact, it hardly matters, since the same measures satisfied both objectives. 'These provisions were critical,' believed the chief US negotiator at the time, Richard Benedick, 'since they constituted in effect the only enforcement mechanism in the Protocol.'[81] 'The specific language of Article 4 itself was less important than the signal it was intended to send to countries which had not responded to repeated invitations to participate in the negotiations or which had refused to ratify the resulting agreement',

---

[80] G. Victor Buxton (Environment Canada), John Temple Lang (European Commission), Steve Lee-Bapty (Department of the Environment), James A. Losey (formerly US EPA), personal communications; Ambassador Winfried Lang (Austria; chair of the Montreal Protocol conference) speaking at the UNEP Ozone Workshop in Vienna, 4 December 1995; Robert A. Reinstein (formerly office of US Trade Representative), 'Experiences with multilateral environmental agreements: lessons for the WTO/GATT', paper presented to T. M. C. Asser Instituut round table conference on the relationship between the multilateral trading system and the use of trade measures in MEAs, The Hague, January 1996.

[81] Benedick, *Ozone Diplomacy*, p. 91.

commented another of the US negotiators later. 'The parties to the Montreal Protocol wished to convince these other countries that they were committed to ensure that the environmental benefits achieved by the Protocol, at some significant cost to the parties, would not be nullified or impaired through operation of the open trading system.'[82]

The negotiations, however, proved that the issue of trade restrictions was highly contentious. The European Community, at the time the biggest producer and exporter of CFCs, was suspicious of US motives, believing they were aimed at creating a competitive advantage for American industry, which was believed to be further advanced in the development of CFC substitutes and also possessed or controlled more production facilities based in developing countries. Further discussion was blocked until an opinion had been obtained from the GATT Secretariat on the compatibility of the proposals with the GATT (see Chapter 4). Once this was obtained, the EC then objected to the Canadian proposal for calculating consumption on the basis of the formula

consumption = production + imports – exports to parties

on the grounds that there was no assurance that their overseas customers would sign the Protocol. Compromise was reached through the agreement, noted above, that the formula would allow the subtraction of *all* exports until 1993. After that date exports to non-parties could not be subtracted and would count against domestic consumption; the EC would thus have both the incentive and the time to persuade its customers to accede.[83] The subsequent success of the Protocol in attracting members made this provision unnecessary and it was amended at London to a simple ban on exports to non-parties.

The delay until 1993 of the ban on imports of products containing ODS, and the agreement simply to study the feasibility of restrictions on imports of goods made with but not containing ODS, were similarly outcomes of a US–EC compromise, to a certain extent of disagreements within the US

---

[82] Reinstein, 'Experiences with MEAs', p. 20.

[83] The decision of the British government to host a conference in March 1989 on 'Saving the ozone layer' and to pay for the attendance of representatives from developing countries can be seen as part of this process.

delegation between negotiators from the EPA and from the US Trade Representative's office,[84] and probably of concern among those negotiators nervous about the implications of these trade restrictions for the GATT (see Chapter 4). Originally the US had proposed the same formula for goods made with but not containing ODS as for products containing ODS – but its negotiators had been unable to prepare sample lists of products, and the speed with which the negotiations were concluded made it impossible to reach complete agreement in these areas, where further discussion in detail was clearly necessary.[85] 'Although these clauses were not airtight,' concluded Benedick, 'cumulatively they constituted a warning that it would be difficult for non-parties to profit from international trade in the controlled substances.'[86]

Effectiveness of the trade provisions: participation

The number of non-parties to the Montreal Protocol is now very small. Significant consumers of ODS not within the Protocol number only Iraq and Mongolia. The only other sizeable countries which have not acceded are Afghanistan, Angola, Burundi, Eritrea, Laos, Madagascar, Rwanda and Somalia, together with eight of the former Soviet republics; but all of these are small consumers and none of them are producers.[87] A number of them have declared their intention to accede to the agreement, and most of the rest have suffered from major political and/or economic disruptions in the recent past.

It is difficult, however, to determine the precise effect of the trade provisions in persuading countries to join the ozone regime. In general, countries have been subject to several incentives to join, including not only fear

---

[84] James A. Losey (formerly US EPA), personal communication.

[85] Patrick Széll, 'Ozone layer and climate change', in H. P. Newhold, W. Lang and K. Zemanek (eds), *Environmental Protection and International Law* (London: Graham & Trotman, 1991), p. 171.

[86] Benedick, *Ozone Diplomacy*, p. 92.

[87] UNEP, *1994 Report of the Economic Options Committee*, p. 6-3; *Status of Ratification / Accession / Acceptance / Approval of the Vienna Convention for the Protection of the Ozone Layer (1985); the Montreal Protocol on Substances that Deplete the Ozone Layer (1987); the London Amendment to the Montreal Protocol (1990); the Copenhagen Amendment to the Montreal Protocol (1992)*, 31 July 1995 (UNEP/OzL./Rat.46).

of trade restrictions, but also a genuine desire to protect the ozone layer, and, for Article 5 countries after 1990, access to the Multilateral Fund and to technology transfer. Disentangling the relative importance of these reasons is impossible. Furthermore, few countries like to admit they have taken a decision through fear of adverse consequences; even if this is their major justification, presenting the move to the outside world as one motivated by environmental considerations is likely to gain more political and diplomatic credit. If access to financial and technical assistance is possible, then it is clearly desirable to present this as the main motivation, in order to maximize future resource transfers.

Having said this, there is general acceptance among participants in and observers of the Montreal Protocol process that the agreement's trade provisions played an important part in the decisions of at least some countries. US threats during the negotiations to apply economic pressure to hesitant countries appear to have impressed some;[88] the US itself was under internal pressure, with bills introduced in Congress during 1986 and 1987 calling for unilateral cuts in CFC production accompanied by trade restrictions against countries which did not reciprocate.[89] Japan in particular is often quoted as a country worried about the prospect of trade sanctions,[90] perhaps seeing them as another attempt by the US to limit Japanese car imports.

The Republic of Korea offers the clearest case. Korea delayed accession to the Protocol until 1992, reportedly because it believed that although it might have benefited from Multilateral Fund assistance, the sums involved would have been hopelessly inadequate to cover the adaptation costs of its large and growing electronics industry (producing exports valued at $13.5 billion in 1989).[91] An estimate of $1.9 billion was produced, compared to

---

[88] Wolfgang Fischer, *The Verification of International Conventions on Protection of the Environment and Common Resources* (Jülich, Germany: Forschungszentrum Jülich, 1991), p. 28.

[89] Parson, 'Protecting the ozone layer', pp. 43, 70.

[90] Cagin and Dray, *Between Earth and Sky*, p. 321; Brenton, *The Greening of Machiavelli*, p. 140.

[91] David O'Connor, *Policy and Entrepreneurial Responses to the Montreal Protocol: Some Evidence from the Dynamic Asian Economies*, OECD Development Centre, Technical Paper 51 (Paris: OECD, 1991), p. 18.

a total Fund size of $240 million for all Article 5 countries over three years.[92] (In fact Korea could not qualify anyway, since it was eventually classified as a non-Article 5 country, its per capita ODS consumption then exceeding 0.3 kg.) Although this is undoubtedly a substantial overestimate, based on the value of lost production if no substitutes were available, it does indicate the magnitude of the perceived costs of accession. Korean domestic ODS production increased in the early years of the Protocol,[93] and the country almost certainly could have reached self-sufficiency. Nevertheless Korea eventually acceded. The threat of trade restrictions by Montreal Protocol signatories (such as the US or EU) against Korean exports such as refrigerators or air-conditioning systems (particularly in cars), or, potentially even worse, against the many Korean electronic goods produced with but not containing ODS, proved a powerful incentive; similarly, the country did not wish to be barred from access to expanding markets in China and elsewhere.

Similar considerations may have influenced the other industrializing countries of South-East Asia, such as Taiwan.[94] In addition to the trade restrictions against non-parties, the application of various policy instruments such as labelling requirements in export markets (see section 3.1) also provided incentives to comply with the control schedules.

Very few developing countries joined the Montreal Protocol at the outset. None at the time were major producers or consumers, and with CFC phase-out originally limited only to 50%, few of them seemed likely to be affected in the foreseeable future. Mexico was a major exception, signing the Protocol at Montreal; the country was experiencing significant investment in electronics plants in the 'maquiladora' free trade zone along its border with the US – another indication of the importance of the trade restrictions. Some developing countries were actively hostile. Malaysia's negotiator at Montreal, for example, criticized the agreement as

---

[92] UNEP, *1994 Report of the Economic Options Committee*, p. 6-3.

[93] Domestic production accounted for 36% of consumption in 1989 and 52% in 1990 (against a fall of 30% in total consumption) *Business Korea*, June 1992, cited in UNEP, *1994 Report of the Economic Options Committee*, p. 6-3.

[94] See *Ozone Layer Protection in Taiwan, ROC* (Hsinchu, Taiwan: Industrial Technology Research Institute / Association of Ozone Layer Protection in Taiwan, 1995), pp. 4, 12.

inequitable, limiting developing countries to a lower per capita consumption level than industrialized countries, and specifically attacked the trade provisions as 'trade war by environmental decree'.[95] More common was the attitude displayed by India, which had shown no interest in the negotiations and 'whose officials in private conversations had characterized the issue as a "rich man's problem – rich man's solution"'.[96] Both India and China at the time were expanding domestic production capacity and seeking new foreign markets; indeed, in 1988 India purchased an entire second-hand CFC-12 plant from Allied Chemical, after the Protocol had been agreed.[97]

This position changed, however, as the growing evidence of serious ozone depletion focused attention on the need for tougher restrictions. The 1990 London Meeting, which discussed and agreed a total phase-out of CFCs and halons, marked a turning point; developing countries, however small their production and consumption, would eventually be cut off from sources of supply and/or face restrictions on their exports if they remained outside the Protocol. The terms under which they would accede thus became a crucial part of the negotiations, resulting in the creation of the Multilateral Fund. While once again it is impossible to disentangle individual developing countries' motivations for joining, most observers accept that the combination of financial assistance and technology transfer plus the fear of trade discrimination created a powerful incentive. When Myanmar, for example, announced its adherence to the Protocol in 1994, its officials stated that one of their major motivations was the desire to avoid trade restrictions.[98] The more countries joined, of course, the greater the incentive for the rest to join too, particularly if there were no significant producers left outside; the trade provisions would then shut off consumers from any legal source of supply and producers from export

---

[95] Abu Bakar, 'Trade war by environmental decree', *Asia Technology,* January 1990, p. 51.
[96] Benedick, *Ozone Diplomacy,* p. 100.
[97] G. Victor Buxton (Environment Canada), personal communication.
[98] 'Burma avoids trade restrictions on CFCs by signing ozone protection agreements', *BBC Monitoring Service, Summary of World Broadcasts,* 12 January 1994, cited in Ian H. Rowlands, *The Politics of Global Atmospheric Change* (Manchester / New York: Manchester University Press, 1995), p. 183.

markets. Moreover, the further development of the ozone regime could only be influenced from the inside.

Effectiveness of the trade provisions: industrial migration

There is no evidence to suggest that industrial migration has occurred to any significant extent in an attempt to escape the control schedules of the Montreal Protocol. Although there are now so few non-parties that this would be almost impossible, it remained a matter of some concern whether ODS-producing industries would move their production facilities to developing countries, which enjoy a longer phase-out period, as phase-out approached in their home countries. This issue forms part of a wider discussion about the propensity of industry to migrate to escape environmental compliance costs and, as in other cases which have been examined, there seems to be virtually no evidence to suggest that this does happen. The decision on where to locate a production facility depends on a whole host of factors, including labour costs, access to markets, social and political conditions, and local infrastructure and regulation. Environmental costs usually play a very small role in these decisions, and in any case environmental regulation is frequently not static; countries identified as so-called 'pollution havens' are not immune to pressure for higher standards.

This is certainly the case with the Montreal Protocol, where even Article 5 countries would only be able to delay implementation of the phase-out schedules for ten years. A TEAP report in 1994 was able to identify only two instances of a shift in industry in response to differential phase-out schedules.[99] In one case a number of relatively small CFC-using enterprises moved their production facilities from Hong Kong (which was subject to the UK phase-out schedule) to Guangdong province in China. Whether they did this to avoid CFC phase-out is not clear; it may well have been in order to gain greater access to Chinese markets, along with many other Hong Kong-based firms. The second case involved a shift in production between different facilities of the same enterprise in different countries,

---

[99] UNEP, *1994 Report of the Economic Options Committee*, p. 6-9.

a development which could be regarded as entirely natural given the changing size of markets in response to ODS phase-out. A study by the UN Conference on Trade and Development (UNCTAD) in Thailand similarly showed an increase in ODS consumption by subsidiaries of transnational companies, or joint ventures with Thai firms.[100] Many developing countries may in fact be reluctant to see this shift proceed too far since, if total production rose as a result above 0.3 kg per capita, the country would lose its Article 5 status and accompanying access to Multilateral Fund support. Malaysia, for example, is now close to the limit and has proved reluctant to admit foreign producers, and Thailand has entered into an understanding with the US and Japanese governments to encourage transnationals to apply the same phase-out schedules in Thailand as in their home countries.

In general, then, there is no evidence to suggest significant industrial migration in order to escape the Montreal Protocol controls.

3.4 The application of the trade provisions

The obligations undertaken by parties to the Montreal Protocol have to be implemented through national legislative systems to ensure that exporters and importers of ODS on their territory do not engage in trade with non-parties. In practice, the gradual evolution of the Protocol through successive rounds of amendments has led to a complex set of trade restrictions between countries at different stages of ratification and phase-out. A non-Article 5 country which had ratified the London and Copenhagen Amendments, for example, would be committed to phasing out production and consumption of Annex B substances (carbon tetrachloride, methyl chloroform and the second group of CFCs) by 1996, banning imports from and exports to non-parties from August 1993. A country which had only ratified the original Montreal Protocol, however (47 countries are currently in this position), would be under no requirement to

---

[100] UNCTAD, *Effects of Environmental Policies, Standards and Regulations on Market Access and Competitiveness, with Special Reference to Developing Countries, including the Least Developed among them, and in the light of UNCTAD Empirical Studies: Environmental Policies, Trade and Competitiveness: Conceptual and Empirical Issues*, 28 March 1995 (TD/B/WG.6/6), paras 103–5.

control production or consumption of, or trade in, any of these substances, which were not covered by the 1987 agreement. The second country should in theory be treated as a non-party by countries which had ratified the later amendments.

In practice, however, although exporters have had to wrestle with complicated matrices of administrative arrangements, this situation does not seem to have caused any major problems for the ozone regime. The big producers of ODS in the industrialized world have moved fast enough to phase out production in harmony with each other; the provisions in the Protocol, and in each of the later amendments, delaying their entry into force until a minimum number of countries had ratified were important in helping to achieve this. In addition, the provision allowing countries to be treated as though they had ratified the Protocol or its amendments if they are in compliance with the appropriate control schedules (regardless of the legal position) has helped to resolve such potential confusions by effectively making it easier for countries to progress through the various stages of the Protocol's evolution (see above).

A similar problem arises with countries which move faster than the requirements of the Protocol. A number of European states, for instance, have declared phase-out dates for HCFCs well in advance of those specified in the Protocol – for example, 2000 in Austria (for major uses), a range of dates (depending on use) between 1996 and 2002 in Denmark, 2000 (for HCFC-22) and 2005 (for other HCFCs) in Germany, and a range between 1994 and 2002 in Sweden. The chemicals industry has been understandably dismayed at facing an increasingly fragmented situation in what is supposed to be a single European market (although not all of these states were EU members when their regulations were decided, they all are now). However, most of these controls are limits on *use,* rather than outright import bans, and there are often exceptions in various instances, so the restriction on trade is not necessarily as severe. In addition, Article 130(t) of the Treaty of Rome, which permits member states to exceed EU minimum standards of environmental protection, together with the 1988 ruling of the European Court of Justice in the Danish bottles case, where regulations effectively restricting trade in carbonated drinks were upheld in the interests of environmental protection, appear to have provided sufficient justification.[101] Sweden certainly felt justified in 1994 in rejecting a European Commission request to bring its HCFC controls – which included a ban on imports from 2000 as well as use controls – into line with (at that time draft) EU legislation in preparation for Swedish accession to the EU.[102] Similarly, in 1990 Sweden introduced a ban on imports of products manufactured with CFCs in the face of criticism from the EC and the European Free Trade Association, EFTA.

The EU itself has in some cases (including CFCs and HCFCs) adopted faster phase-out schedules than required by the Protocol, but has proved sensitive to particular problems thus caused. In 1993, for example, the EU exempted a number of countries from the trade restrictions on methyl chloroform which it would otherwise have imposed.[103] Strict controls on methyl bromide are also becoming more widespread. Denmark, Norway, Sweden and Finland are all scheduled to ban domestic use (and therefore imports) by 1998, and Austria by 2000; from 1 January 1995, New Zealand restricted imports to 1991 levels (which represents roughly a 20% cut), except where use is for quarantine and pre-shipment purposes.

3.5 Conclusion: the importance of the trade provisions

All else being equal, restrictions on the free exchange of goods across international borders should result in a welfare loss. Trade restrictions pursuant to MEAs must therefore provide counter-justifications. There are two.

First, trade measures can reduce the extent of free-riding, where non-signatories benefit from the actions taken by signatories without incurring any costs themselves. The objective of maximizing participation in the Protocol was one aim of the trade provisions, and the international regime put in place through the Vienna Convention and the Montreal Protocol and its subsequent amendments, including the restrictions on trade described above, has proved remarkably effective in attracting adherents on a global scale.

---

[101] Nick Campbell (ICI Klea), personal communication.

[102] *Global Environmental Change Report* VI:5, 11 March 1994, p. 4.

[103] Nick Campbell (ICI Klea), personal communication.

Second, trade measures can reduce leakage, the situation where non-signatories increase their emissions as a result of the control measures taken by signatories. This was the other aim of the negotiators in Montreal: to prevent industrial migration, and non-signatories gaining a competitive advantage. Once again this appears to have been successful: there is no evidence at all to suggest that countries are staying outside the Montreal Protocol in a deliberate attempt to evade the control schedules, thus posing a threat to the ozone layer.

A theoretical study by the economist Scott Barrett supports the use of trade restrictions in MEAs.[104] Employing a model of international trade and pollution in which identical firms choose how much of a good to produce and ship to each market and identical governments choose allowable emission levels, Barrett found that a ban on imports from non-signatories of the agreement to signatories, and a partial restriction on exports from signatories to non-signatories, could be credible and possibly severe enough to deter free-riding completely, though these restrictions would not necessarily sustain full cooperation. Importantly, he found that cooperation was never partial – i.e. total and zero participation were the two equilibrium points of the model – and therefore trade was never restricted in practice. 'It is the credible *threat* of employing trade restrictions which can sustain full cooperation in environmental protection.'[105]

The balance between the benefits of increasing cooperation and reducing leakage, and the costs of forgone gains from trade, is obviously struck more positively the higher the level of participation. As the theory suggests, participation in the Montreal Protocol is now almost universal and threats from leakage or free-riding are negligible – and therefore the trade provisions do not need to be implemented. The tendency towards total participation is encouraged by the provision that the agreement does not come into force until a certain minimum number of countries representing an

---

[104] Scott Barrett, *Trade Restrictions in International Environmental Agreements*, Centre for Social and Economic Research on the Global Environment Working Paper GEC 94-13, 1994, and Scott Barrett, 'Trade restrictions in international environmental agreements: the case of the Montreal Protocol', paper prepared for OECD joint session of trade and environment experts, 24 January 1995 (COM/ENV/TD(95)15).

[105] Barrett, *Trade Restrictions,* p. 31.

agreed percentage of world production and consumption have signed.[106]

The trade provisions of the Montreal Protocol are therefore entirely justifiable in terms of the aim of the agreement: the protection of the ozone layer. Indeed, they appear to have been a vital component in the success of the agreement. The trade measures need, however, to be *credible:*

- They should not change so rapidly – through the evolution of the control measures via successive amendments and adjustments – that countries find themselves unable to comply with the accelerated phase-outs, and feel compelled to reinstate or expand domestic production, and/or turn to the black market for supplies. This is a fine balance to strike, but so far the parties to the Montreal Protocol appear to have achieved it. Particular concerns arise in the case of developing countries, and are considered in Chapter 5.
- The trade measures should also be effective; they should punish countries which do not cooperate and reward those which do. Problems arising from evasion of the controls are examined in Chapter 6.
- The restrictions on trade mandated by the Montreal Protocol should not be liable to be undermined by other aspects of international law – specifically, the world trading regime established by the GATT and the WTO. It is to this aspect that we turn next.

---

[106] Article 16 of the Montreal Protocol specified that the agreement would enter into force on 1 January 1989 provided that at least 11 countries representing at least two-thirds of global consumption had ratified it.

Chapter 4

The Montreal Protocol and the world trading system

The relationship between the legal structures of the international trading system and of MEAs such as the Montreal Protocol is central to the current debate on trade and environment. If the twin but sometimes conflicting aims of trade liberalization and environmental protection cannot be reconciled through MEAs, then the international community is likely to be faced with continuing friction and antagonism as global environmental problems worsen. This chapter examines the issue of the compatibility of the Montreal Protocol and the GATT and its governing institution, the WTO.

4.1 GATT and the environment

The central aim of the GATT is to liberalize trade between contracting parties. Its core principles are to be found in Article I ('most favoured nation' treatment), Article III ('national treatment') and Article XI ('elimination of quantitative restrictions'). Article I requires that any trade advantage granted by any contracting party to any product either for import or export must also be applied to any 'like product' originating in or bound for any other contracting party. Article III similarly requires imported and domestic 'like products' to be treated identically with respect to internal taxes and regulations. WTO members, in other words, are not permitted to discriminate between traded products produced by other WTO members, or between domestic and international products. Article XI forbids any restrictions other than duties, taxes or other charges on imports from and exports to other contracting parties.

The requirements of the Montreal Protocol would appear to carry the potential to bring parties into conflict with these provisions. The control measures in Article 2 can lead to restrictions on imports of ODS and products containing ODS from other parties to the Protocol (see section 3.1). The trade restrictions in Article 4 instruct parties to ban imports from, and exports to, non-parties of ODS, of products containing ODS, and, potentially, of goods made with but not containing ODS. In all these cases, if the parties or non-parties concerned are WTO members, this is discriminatory behaviour.

The GATT does permit, however, certain unilateral trade restrictions in the pursuit of environmental protection under particular circumstances. Article XX ('General Exceptions') states that:

> Subject to the requirement that such measures are not applied in a manner which would constitute a means of arbitrary or unjustifiable discrimination between countries where the same conditions prevail, or a disguised restriction on international trade, nothing in this Agreement shall be construed to prevent the adoption or enforcement by any contracting party of measures:
>
> . . .
>
> (b) necessary to protect human, animal or plant life or health;
>
> . . .
>
> (g) relating to the conservation of exhaustible natural resources if such measures are made effective in conjunction with restrictions on domestic production or consumption.

Either of these clauses could be used to justify some restrictions on trade in ODS or in products containing ODS. As the GATT Secretariat stated in 1992, 'GATT rules, therefore, place essentially no constraints on a country's right to protect its own environment against damage from either domestic production or the consumption of domestically produced or imported products. Generally speaking, a country can do anything to imports or exports that it does to its own products, and it can do anything it considers necessary to its own production processes.'[107]

Countries can, therefore, ban the import of products which will harm their own environments, *as long as the standards applied are non-discriminatory between countries and between domestic and foreign production.* The GATT Agreement on Technical Barriers to Trade (TBT) aims to

---

[107] *International Trade 1990–91* (Geneva: GATT Secretariat, 1992), p. 23.

encourage international harmonization of product standards and to avoid their use for disguised protectionism. Under para. 2.2 of the Agreement, technical regulations shall not be more trade restrictive than necessary to fulfil a 'legitimate objective' – which is defined as including environmental protection. (The clause in the Montreal Protocol exempting non-parties from trade measures if they can show themselves to be in compliance with the phase-out schedules is important in this respect, demonstrating that the trade restrictions are based on legitimate environmental objectives and not merely on formal membership of an international agreement.) Environmental grounds have become more widely cited as an objective and rationale for applying technical regulations under the TBT Agreement, including, most notably, measures aimed at controlling air pollution and hazardous chemicals, including ODS.[108]

4.2 GATT and the Montreal Protocol

The negotiations

The issue of the Protocol's compatibility with the GATT was raised during the original negotiations. A sub-group established by the Ad Hoc Working Group of Legal and Technical Experts provisionally concluded that the proposed trade measures could be justifiable under Article XX(b), and possibly XX(g), of the GATT. The members of the group had in mind the precedent of the Convention on International Trade in Endangered Species (CITES), an agreement whose main aim was the application of trade restrictions. Since its negotiation in 1973 no GATT contracting party had ever objected to its provisions, implying its acceptability under public international law.[109] Similarly, the proposed trade measures of the Montreal Protocol would be applied pursuant to a *multilateral* international agreement, and not on a unilateral, ad hoc basis. This was an important consideration, according to at least one observer.[110] The main guiding ethos of the GATT agreement is an antipathy towards unilateral action, which is seen, understandably, as risking retaliatory protectionism. Although Article XX

---

[108] Ibid., p. 32.

[109] John Temple Lang (European Commission), personal communication.

[110] Patrick Széll (Department of the Environment), personal communication.

does permit WTO members to take unilateral action in pursuit of environmental ends, the circumstances are carefully defined, and the actions are subject to challenge under the GATT/WTO disputes procedures. By staying within a multilateral framework, the Montreal Protocol did not appear to threaten this structure.

Controls on products containing ODS – and, even more, on products made with but not containing ODS – were, however, seen by at least some of the negotiators as probably less consistent with the GATT. The delay in the implementation of these provisions that finally occurred (see Chapter 3) gave an opportunity for further consideration and, possibly, non-implementation should the ozone regime prove successful without them.

Consultations were held with a legal expert from the GATT Secretariat in April and September 1987. No definite opinion was given; the expert provided advice as to whether particular language was relatively closer to or further away from traditional interpretations of the GATT. The GATT lawyer stressed that 'the judgement as to whether a proposed action to implement the trade restrictions satisfied Article XX lay with GATT Contracting Parties normally in the context of a complaint by one GATT Party against another'.[111] This opinion was not given in writing,[112] and although the Secretariat in Geneva was presented with an advance copy of the proposed trade provisions, it did not produce a formal response.[113] This was standard practice for the GATT Secretariat, which (unlike the secretariats of many other international organizations) did not regard itself as possessing powers to interpret, or even advise on, its governing agreement.

It has to be remembered, however, that at this time – early 1987 – no governments, and relatively few individuals, involved in the discussions foresaw this as a major potential area of dispute. Indeed, the whole issue

---

[111] 'Report of the Ad Hoc Working Group on the Work of its Third Session', cited in Rosalind Twum-Barima and Laura B. Campbell, *Protecting the Ozone Layer through Trade Measures: Reconciling the Trade Provisions of the Montreal Protocol and the Rules of the GATT* (Geneva: UNEP, 1994), p. 63.

[112] Patrick Széll (Department of the Environment), personal communication.

[113] Twum-Barima and Campbell, *Protecting the Ozone Layer through Trade Measures,* p. 63, n. 113.

of the interaction between trade liberalization and environmental protection was not then considered as important as it is today. The GATT had established a working group on environmental measures and international trade (the 'EMIT group') as far back as 1971, but it remained completely inactive until 1991; environmental policy was simply not seen, either by the GATT or by trade ministries in general, as an important problem, among other reasons because no objections under GATT had ever been made to the well-known and widely ratified CITES treaty mentioned above. For their part, the Montreal Protocol negotiators had no desire to erect unnecessary obstacles to the progress they were otherwise making, and most did not believe in any case that there was likely to be any problem with compatibility. The lack of any formal objection from the GATT Secretariat, however qualified its advice, was seen as a green light for further negotiations, helping the US to convince the EU of the value of the proposed trade measures (see section 3.3). [114]

The Open-Ended Working Group of the Montreal Protocol discussed problems relating to the implementation of the trade provisions in 1990, and came to much the same conclusion as the negotiators had with regard to the GATT. While by that stage convinced that trade restrictions on products containing ODS were justified, the main area of concern they identified was the problem of justifying trade restrictions under the GATT on products produced with but not containing ODS if it proved to be difficult to distinguish the goods in the absence of trace residues (see section 3.2). [115]

Subsequent developments

Since the original negotiations, however, the trade restrictions have grown to occupy a more important role in the Montreal Protocol, and the issue of compatibility with the GATT has been considered more actively. Major concern has been caused by the reports of two GATT disputes panels, in 1991 and 1994, on trade measures taken by the US in the tuna-dolphin dis-

---

[114] James A. Losey (formerly US EPA), personal communication.
[115] Twum-Barima and Campbell, *Protecting the Ozone Layer through Trade Measures*, pp. 62–3; Benedick, *Ozone Diplomacy*, p. 91.

Box 4.1: The tuna-dolphin disputes

In the late 1980s fishing fleets, mainly from Mexico, caught and killed about 30,000 dolphins a year in the process of harvesting tuna in the eastern tropical Pacific Ocean, where dolphins and tuna swim together. In 1991 the US government, acting under the provisions of the Marine Mammal Protection Act, banned imports of tuna and tuna products from Mexico on the grounds that the Mexican dolphin-kill ratio was more than 1.25 times that of US fishermen. Mexico argued that its right to sell tuna in the US had been violated and asked for a GATT dispute panel to rule on the matter. In September 1991 the panel found that the US was indeed in violation of its obligations under GATT, on the following grounds:

- The US kill-ratio standard was inappropriate as it was retroactively determined. It was based on the US fishing fleet's dolphin-kill ratio in any given year, and therefore it was impossible for the Mexicans to know in advance the target at which they had to aim. This was in many ways the strongest argument against the import ban, suggesting blatantly protectionist intent.

- The ban violated the GATT 'like product' provisions, since it did not ban *all* tuna, but only that caught by Mexicans. The panel argued that while GATT members are entitled to ban imports of *products* which are themselves environmentally harmful (so long as domestic production of the same products is also banned), it was not the tuna itself which caused the damage in this case, but the *way* in which it was caught – and trade measures based on such 'process and production methods' (PPMs) not related to the characteristics of the product could *not* be justified under the GATT.

- The action could not be justified under Article XX of the GATT, as neither of the 'saving' clauses (b) or (g) in Article XX could be applied unilaterally outside US jurisdiction. (The panel actually used the word 'extrajurisdictionality', a term which it invented but did not define: it can presumably be taken to refer to a law concerning activities occurring outside the jurisdiction of the country in question.)

- The trade ban could also not be justified under Article XX(b) because the panel believed that it was not *necessary* to the objective: less trade-restrictive measures than a trade embargo were available (such as the negotiation of an international agreement on dolphin conservation) and could have been pursued.

On only one point was the US found to be in accordance with the GATT: the introduction of a 'dolphin-safe' labelling scheme, which was non-discriminatory in that it applied to tuna caught by any fisherman.

In fact, Mexico did not pursue the case, since it did not want to prejudice the outcome of the negotiations on the North American Free Trade Agreement (NAFTA) then under way. The panel ruling was therefore never adopted by the GATT Council, but it has had a significant influence on subsequent debate and has clearly influenced thinking on the trade–environment interaction.

The issue came to the fore once again because of the US 'intermediary nation embargo', banning imports of tuna and tuna products from countries which had in the previous six months imported tuna and tuna products which would have been refused entry to the US; Costa Rica, Italy, Japan and Spain were affected. In 1992 the EC (and the Netherlands, since the Dutch Antilles had been affected under an earlier and wider definition of the embargo) requested a disputes panel to rule on the trade restrictions.

The second panel reported in 1994 and once again found against the US action, though this time on slightly different grounds. The panel's findings differed from the earlier decision mainly in that the second panel was more prepared to accept that the provisions of Article XX(g) could be applied to policies related to the conservation of natural resources outside the territory of the country in question. This was solely an interpretation of the GATT itself, however; the panel did not believe that it could take into account the international environmental agreements (including the Montreal Protocol) cited by the US in its defence as precedents for trade restrictions.

The panel believed, however, that the wording of the article implied that measures could be justified only if they were 'primarily aimed at' rendering effective the restrictions on domestic production, in terms of *both* purpose *and* effect, and that 'measures taken so as to force other countries to change their policies, and that were effective only if such changes occurred, could not be primarily aimed at either the conservation of an exhaustible natural resource, or at rendering effective restrictions on domestic production or consumption in the meaning of Article XX(g).'[116] In terms of Article XX(b), the panel argued similarly that the trade embargoes were not 'necessary' for the protection of animal life or health.

The panel concluded by observing that it 'had ... to resolve whether the contracting parties, by agreeing to give each other in Article XX the right to take trade measures necessary to protect the health and life of plants, animals and persons or aimed at the conservation of exhaustible natural resources, had agreed to accord each other the right to impose trade embargoes for such purposes. The Panel had examined the issue in the light of the recognized methods of interpretation and had found that none of them lent any support to the view that such an agreement was reflected in Article XX.'[117] This is a hugely sweeping statement; if accepted, it is difficult to see what scope would remain for WTO members to use any unilateral measure at all to protect the environment, whether domestic or global.

Like the earlier report, however, this one was not adopted by the GATT Council – primarily because the NAFTA negotiations, particularly on its environmental side-agreement, had still not been concluded. It is worth noting that under the WTO's new disputes settlement procedure, panel findings are adopted *unless* a consensus decides otherwise – the reverse of the GATT mechanism – making it much more likely that panel reports will be adopted.

---

[116] US: Restrictions on Tuna (1994): Report of the Panel, para. 5.27.

[117] Ibid., para. 5.42.

putes. The findings of the panels, summarized in Box 4.1, significantly changed the context in which the debate was held.

Whatever the weaknesses of the US case in the tuna-dolphin dispute, the reports of the two panels appeared to cast considerable doubts over the GATT-compatibility of the Montreal Protocol. Its control measures lead to quantitative restrictions on trade; its trade provisions directed against non-parties can be applied against WTO members who are not Protocol signatories, and envisage trade restrictions on the basis of process and production methods (PPMs); and both sets of measures could be regarded as extrajurisdictional.

Before moving on to examine these specific points of potential conflict, however, it must be remembered that no dispute has in fact arisen within the GATT or WTO over the application of trade restrictions under the Protocol. Partly this is a result of the very wide membership achieved by the Protocol – wider, indeed, than the WTO itself, with 150 members compared to 110 for the WTO in October 1995 – since most of the potential for trade conflict arises with non-members of the Protocol (though the Protocol's membership was initially much smaller). Partly, however, it is also almost certainly due to a genuine desire not to create unnecessary conflict. Although the two agreements do appear to conflict with each other, the world community is committed to them both, and wishes to see them both succeed, and therefore wishes to avoid bringing conflicts to the level of formal disputes mechanisms. This is not to imply, however, that conflicts may never arise in the future, particularly when considered in the context of other MEAs.

4.3 GATT and the Montreal Protocol: areas of incompatibility[118]

Where are the precise areas of conflict between the Montreal Protocol and the GATT? If Article XX of the GATT is to be used to justify the Protocol's trade provisions, then they must be able to satisfy the conditions laid down in its headnote: that is, they should not 'constitute a

---

[118] The information in this section is taken very largely from Twum-Barima and Campbell, *Protecting the Ozone Layer through Trade Measures,* pp. 63–72.

means of arbitrary or unjustifiable discrimination between countries where the same conditions prevail', or a 'disguised restriction on international trade'. If qualifying under Article XX(g), they must be 'relating to the conservation of exhaustible natural resources, if such measures are made effective in conjunction with restrictions on domestic production or consumption'; if under Article XX(b), they must be 'necessary to protect human, animal or plant life or health'. Finally, there is the matter of trade measures based on PPMs.

Arbitrary and unjustifiable discrimination

Since parties to the Montreal Protocol are required to limit their consumption and production of ODS, while non-parties are bound by no such requirement, the same conditions do not exist for parties and non-parties. Therefore, it can be argued, the discrimination entailed in the trade restrictions is neither arbitrary nor unjustifiable. This argument is strengthened by the fact that non-parties which nevertheless comply with the control schedules are treated as if they were parties – i.e. it is not the formal membership of the agreement which determines their treatment, but the degree to which they accept and implement its terms. In addition, the Multilateral Fund provides a mechanism for compensating eligible parties for any welfare loss due to restrictions on trade.

Disguised restriction on trade

The terms of the Montreal Protocol are entirely transparent, both in their international and domestic application, and the trade measures are explicitly aimed at restricting trade between parties and non-parties. There is, therefore, no disguised restriction. A possible alternative interpretation of this phrase would require an examination of the degree of protectionist intent of the measures – but this has not been the approach of GATT panels so far.[119]

---

[119] For a fuller discussion of this argument, see Steve Charnovitz, 'Exploring the environmental exceptions in GATT Article XX', *Journal of World Trade* 25:5, October 1991, pp. 47–8.

Relating to the conservation of exhaustible natural resources

Does the ozone layer, or the atmosphere as a whole, represent a 'natural resource' within the meaning of the terms of the GATT? It has been argued that natural resources in this context should be defined as those of economic value rather than those which cannot be economically exploited, which would appear to rule out the ozone layer. However, given the economic costs which arise from ozone depletion, this is not a strong argument, and is distinctly out of tune with scientific and diplomatic thinking over recent years. The GATT disputes panel in the second tuna-dolphin case interpreted the phrase 'relating to' to mean primarily aimed at conserving the natural resource in question, and since dolphins are not in general economically exploitable and the Montreal Protocol is clearly aimed at conserving the ozone layer, the Protocol's trade provisions would almost certainly satisfy this section of the GATT.

The territorial application of trade measures taken in pursuit of environmental goals is the main area of dispute under this heading. Both tuna-dolphin disputes panels found against the US actions partly on the grounds that they attempted to determine or influence the policies of other GATT members. This objection could also be applied to exemptions sought under Article XX(b) (see below) as well as XX(g). Whether this would still be applicable in the context of an MEA aimed at protecting the global environment is less clear, though the second panel's finding that trade measures contained in MEAs such as the Montreal Protocol did not provide a sufficient precedent suggests that it might.

Necessity of trade measures for the protection of life and health

This is probably the most difficult area. The terms of the Montreal Protocol, drawn up and revised with constant reference to scientific assessments of the extent and costs of ozone depletion, and the relative costs and benefits of abatement actions, could certainly be regarded as qualifying under a scientific test of the necessity of the measures taken. However, in recent years GATT disputes panels and reports have progressively narrowed the scope of the 'necessity' exemption, interpreting it increasingly as 'least GATT-inconsistent' or 'least trade-restrictive'. This behaviour is reinforced by other elements of the GATT, such as the TBT Agreement, which includes the requirement that 'technical regulations shall not be more trade-restrictive than necessary to fulfil a legitimate objective' (which includes environmental protection). [120]

The question then arises whether any alternatives to the Protocol's trade provisions were available which would have achieved the same objective in a less trade-restrictive way. This is in many ways the key to the debate over the relationship between the GATT and MEAs. Although the GATT Secretariat has repeatedly stressed that it has neither the desire nor the expertise to interfere in international environmental policy, it has nevertheless questioned the necessity of MEAs to affect trading relations between WTO members. Admitting the possibility of conflict between GATT rules and MEAs with trade provisions, the 1992 GATT report on trade and the environment suggested that 'it is not clear that such departures from the non-discrimination principle are always necessary to achieve the environmental goals of the environmental agreement.'[121] In February 1996 Richard Eglin, Director of the WTO Trade and Environment Division, publicly reaffirmed this position, and questioned both the necessity and the efficacy of the Montreal Protocol's trade provisions.[122]

Two main alternatives to the existing trade provisions have been suggested. The first is the application of controls on consumption through economic instruments such as taxes, which would still permit the users to buy from any source, domestic or foreign; the taxes would have to be applied at the border for imports from non-parties. In theory, taxes could be applied either at the point where the ODS are emitted into the atmosphere (i.e. at the point of disposal or use), or at the point of incorporation into products, or at the point of production. Only a handful of countries, however, have so far introduced such taxes (see Chapter 3). They suffer from a number of problems. There are formidable technical difficulties in identifying both the appropriate tax rates at different stages of phase-out

---

[120] GATT Agreement on Technical Barriers to Trade, Article 2.2.

[121] GATT Secretariat, *International Trade 1990–91*, p. 25.

[122] House of Commons Environment Committee, inquiry into world trade and the environment, evidence session of 14 February 1996.

and the products to which they should be applied, particularly where these are imported. The impact of taxation on the reduction of pollution cannot be precisely known, rendering it a difficult instrument to employ in meeting quantitative control targets. As discussed below, taxes imposed on products produced with, but not containing, ODS, could fall foul of the GATT's 'like product' provisions. Furthermore, at the time that the Montreal Protocol was negotiated the concept of environmental taxes, now more widely accepted, was in its infancy. It was essential to unite all the negotiating countries, including the centrally planned economies, in the agreement. Serious doubts would almost certainly have existed about the ability and willingness of some of the parties to the Protocol (particularly the non-market-based economies of the Soviet bloc) to introduce and collect internationally mandated taxes.[123] Even today, Western governments' treasury departments are hardly enthusiastic proponents of this approach.

Finally, taxes imposed on imports would not necessarily discourage the use of ODS in exporting non-parties, particularly where the bulk of ODS production there was intended for domestic consumption. In many ways, this is the crucial objection to market-based instruments. Although in theory they are more economically efficient than simple production and consumption caps, the *environmental* efficiency of the control measures depends in large part on their international coverage. As discussed in Chapter 3, although it is impossible to be precise about the incentive effects of the trade provisions, it seems highly unlikely that *removing* the threat of cutting off supplies of ODS to non-parties would have made these countries *more* likely to join the Protocol. As UNEP's *Economic Options Report* put it, 'it has been argued that . . . the same reductions could have been achieved at lower cost through the use of more efficient instruments in countries that are parties to the Protocol than through trade sanctions on "free riders". This is probably true *ex post* (because there are so few free riders) but that may be because the *threat* of trade sanctions has brought so many countries into the Protocol. It is impossible to resolve such a debate

---

[123] See Alice Enders and Amelia Porges, 'Successful conventions and conventional success: saving the ozone layer', in Kym Anderson and Richard Blackhurst, *The Greening of World Trade Issues* (London: Harvester Wheatsheaf, 1992), pp. 133–4.

on economic grounds.'[124] Despite these major reservations, some on the trade side of the debate still maintain that taxes should have been introduced in preference to the existing provisions.[125]

The second major alternative to the trade provisions that has been suggested is an outright ban on imports from any country, which would not discriminate between parties and non-parties to the Protocol and would therefore be less inconsistent with the GATT.[126] Once again, however, this suffers from severe practical difficulties. The number of ODS producers was, and is, so limited that a complete import ban would cut off the majority of ODS consumers from their sources of supply. This would if anything create a powerful incentive for non-producers to stay outside the Protocol and either import from other non-parties or set up their own domestic production facilities. It would also increase the likelihood of ODS-producing industries migrating to non-parties, and help to undermine the competitive position of parties. Finally, such a proposal would almost certainly have deterred the EU, then the world's major exporter, from agreeing to the original Protocol in 1987.[127]

The question of the necessity of the Protocol's trade provisions is probably the area of most vulnerability to challenge under the GATT – but only because GATT disputes panels have adopted such a narrow view of the meaning of the term 'necessary'. The first panel ruling on the US–Mexico tuna-dolphin dispute, for example, found against the US import ban partly because unilateral actions were more GATT-inconsistent than the negotiation of international agreements – entirely regardless of the political feasibility of negotiating such agreements. Similarly, the problems associated with the alternatives to the trade provisions discussed above, which relate

---

[124] UNEP, *1994 Report of the Economic Options Committee*, pp. 6-4–6-5.

[125] See, for example, Markus Schlagenhof, 'Trade measures based on environmental processes and production methods', *Journal of World Trade* 29:6, December 1995, p. 149, and GATT Secretariat, *International Trade 1990–91*, p. 25.

[126] A complete import ban would still violate Article XI of the GATT ('elimination of quantitative restrictions') but could have been 'saved' under Article XX, subject to the arguments in the preceding paragraphs.

[127] For a scathing attack on a suggestion of import bans made by the GATT Secretariat, see John Temple Lang, 'The problem was already solved: GATT Panels and public international law', paper presented to Dublin Conference of International Bar Association / Irish Centre for European Law, November 1994.

to administrative practicality, political feasibility and environmental effectiveness, could well be completely ignored by a future WTO disputes panel sticking only to the narrow issue of the impact on trade.[128] In effect, the panels have pretended to operate in the 'first-best' world of economic theory, where trade losses automatically translate into welfare losses. Unfortunately the real world does not often behave like that, partly because as yet most environmental externalities – such as the costs of ozone depletion – are not incorporated into economic prices and decisions. The story of ozone depletion and the evolution of the Montreal Protocol itself reveals how dangerous such narrow world views can be.

Trade measures based on process and production methods

The GATT's 'like product' provisions in Articles I and III were designed to prevent a country discriminating against imports on the basis of their territorial origin. They were not drawn up with environmental arguments in mind, but the tuna-dolphin panels applied them anyway, interpreting the definition of 'like product' to cover products which are the same even if the way in which they are produced is different. In 1994, another GATT panel, ruling on the EU–US dispute over the application of taxes to imports of EU cars into the US on the basis of fuel efficiency standards, slightly relaxed the definition of 'like product'. It considered that vehicles of different fuel efficiency standards could be considered not to be 'like products'. However, it placed strict boundaries on this conclusion, arguing that Article III of the GATT referred only to a 'product as a product, from its introduction into the market to its final consumption'.[129] Factors relating to the manufacture of the product before its introduction into the market were still, therefore, irrelevant.

Even if one does not adopt the panels' viewpoints, PPM-based environmental trade measures can be difficult to justify. PPMs are often highly country-specific. Different parts of the world vary widely in their ability to assimilate pollution, depending on factors such as climate, population den-

---

[128] See Brack, 'Balancing trade and the environment', p. 512.
[129] US: Taxes on Automobiles (1994): Report of the Panel, para. 5.52.

sity, existing levels of pollution and risk preferences. Environmental regulations suited to industrialized nations, with high population densities and environments which have been subject to pollution for the last 200 years, may be wholly inappropriate for newly industrializing countries with much lower population densities and inherited pollution levels – and yet trade measures based on PPMs could in effect seek to impose the higher standards regardless. Carried to its logical extreme, enforcing similarity of PPMs could deny the very basis of comparative advantage, which rests on the proposition that countries possess different cost structures for the production of various goods. Another argument rests on practicalities. By their very nature, PPMs cannot generally be determined by inspection of their products. Importers wishing to apply PPM-based controls must therefore enjoy the cooperation of the exporting country or country of origin in certifying how the goods are produced.

These arguments, if accepted, would appear to rule out any action taken in respect of the Montreal Protocol provisions with regard to products 'produced with, but not containing' ODS. As described in Chapter 3, the Protocol requires the parties to determine the feasibility of banning or restricting imports of such products from non-parties. Although the parties have so far decided that such trade restrictions are not feasible, due primarily to technical problems of detection, it is not impossible that these problems could be solved eventually; the question is scheduled for regular review. Furthermore, it seems likely that the threat of such potential restrictions did encourage a number of countries to join the regime. This provision cannot therefore be written off as a dead letter, even with regard to the Montreal Protocol (see the discussion concerning methyl bromide in section 3.2), let alone future MEAs.

The panels' finding against PPM-based trade measures can, however, be challenged. The prohibition of PPM-based trade measures is nowhere stated in the GATT text. In other areas of the GATT the distinction between products and PPMs is not maintained. Both the Agreement on Subsidies and Countervailing Measures and the Agreement on Trade-Related Aspects of Intellectual Property Rights regulate some aspects of *how* goods are produced, allowing importing countries to discriminate against products if they are produced using excessive subsidy or misappropriated intellectual property. GATT's Article XX(e) allows countries to discriminate against products produced using prison labour. Furthermore, the panels' decisions appeared to contradict GATT's first (1971) report on trade and environment, which stated that a 'shared resource, such as a lake or the atmosphere, which is being polluted by foreign producers may give rise to restrictions on trade in the product of that process justifiable on grounds of the public interest in the importing country of control over a process carried out in an adjacent or nearby country'.[130]

An important difference arises between PPMs which cause pollution that is restricted to the country of production, and those which cause pollution that is transboundary or global – such as PPMs using ODS. In the latter case, differentiating, as the panels' interpretation of the GATT does, between pollution associated with the *consumption* of a product and that associated with its *production* is absurd. PPMs which release ODS into the atmosphere deplete the ozone layer, and therefore harm the importing country, whatever part of the world it is in, and wherever in the world the ODS are produced, not because of the *import,* but because of the effect on the ozone layer. By importing, the country in question would contribute to the world demand for products whose production damages the global environment, with varying effects upon individual countries. Certainly this is what the Montreal Protocol negotiators appear to have believed when drawing up the PPM clause.[131]

It is possible that the panel's underlying objection to the US tuna ban was founded not on the use of PPMs per se, but on the spectre of unilateral action that it appeared to raise, which has always been regarded as anathema to the foundations of the GATT. If this is true, the application of PPM-based trade measures in pursuit of a multilateral agreement could prove more acceptable. In any case, extrapolations of arguments based on fishing practices are a poor way to handle trade restrictions aimed at protecting the Earth's stratospheric ozone layer.

---

[130] Quoted in Steve Charnovitz, 'GATT and the environment: examining the issues', *International Environmental Affairs* 4:3, Summer 1992, p. 204.
[131] John Temple Lang (European Commission), personal communication.

4.4 Conclusion: resolving the incompatibilities

There are, clearly, a number of reasons for believing that the trade provisions of the Montreal Protocol (including the so far unimplemented controls on goods produced with but not containing ODS) could be open to challenge under the terms of the GATT, since it could be argued that they violate Article I ('most favoured nation' treatment), Article III ('national treatment') and/or Article XI ('elimination of quantitative restrictions'). Since neither of the tuna-dolphin panel rulings was adopted by the GATT Council, however, it is not clear what interpretation would be upheld by the full WTO membership; and in the absence of a direct challenge to the Protocol's trade provisions, and a subsequent WTO panel ruling, it will remain unclear, though it does seem unlikely that any challenge would succeed.

This is, however, an undesirable situation, for (at least) three reasons. First, industry remains concerned about the possibility, however small, that the trade provisions might be struck down and the control schedules consequently undermined; as seen in Chapter 3, trade restrictions were viewed as helpful in the development of CFC substitutes. Second, the unlaid ghost of a GATT challenge to the Montreal Protocol cannot encourage the introduction of similar trade provisions in future MEAs – yet, as we have seen, their existence was vital to the success of the Protocol and may be equally so to other agreements.[132] Third, the perception that the GATT regime threatens environmental sustainability – already widespread in some quarters – assists neither the growth of the WTO nor the further spread of trade liberalization, even where this would have environmental benefits.

A resolution of the problem is therefore highly desirable, and the question has been under discussion since before the UN Conference on Environment and Development in Rio in 1992.[133] Now much more widely

---

[132] It has been suggested that the threat of GATT challenges has already been deployed in opposition to various aspects of other MEAs, including the Climate Change Convention: James Cameron (Foundation for International Environmental Law and Development), personal communication.

[133] See, e.g., James Cameron and Jonathan Robinson, 'The use of trade provisions in international environmental agreements and their compatibility with the GATT', *Yearbook of International Environmental Law*, 1991, vol. 2 (London: Graham & Trotman, 1991).

accep῾ on the international agenda, the topic is currently being consid-
er῾ the WTO's Committee on Trade and Environment. In principle
er῾ are a number of ways in which the potential incompatibility between
the GATT and MEAs with trade provisions could be resolved. Three in
particular stand out.

First and most ambitiously, the GATT could be amended to include a
new 'sustainability clause' setting out agreed principles of environmental
policy – such as the polluter pays principle and the precautionary principle[134] – against which trade measures can be judged. This is similar in concept to clauses (r), (s) and (t) of Article 130 of the Treaty of Rome, which
enable EU institutions to pursue *both* trade liberalization *and* environmental sustainability as objectives. As the EU has shown, conflict between
these two objectives can be resolved successfully, striking a balance appropriate to the particular circumstances.[135]

Second, the GATT could be amended to create a presumption of compatibility with MEAs, by means of an extension of the exemptions set out
in Article XX to permit trade measures pursuant to MEAs.[136] This is similar in concept to the clause in NAFTA which specifically allows that, in
most cases where conflict arises between its own provisions and those of
the Montreal Protocol, the Basel Convention or CITES (or future MEAs
where the NAFTA parties agree), the MEA shall prevail – though it would
be undesirable to restrict the application of the new GATT clause simply
to three MEAs. Examples put forward by the EU for discussion in the
WTO include an amendment to Article XX(b) of the GATT to include specific mention of the environment, and/or a new sub-paragraph in Article
XX listing measures taken pursuant to an MEA.[137]

Third, the GATT already contains a waiver clause (in Article XXV)
which would permit the contracting parties to decide on a case-by-case
basis to waive any sections of the GATT which were felt to be incompatible
with MEAs.

---

[134] Vital to the negotiation of the Montreal Protocol: see Chapter 3.

[135] See Brack, 'Balancing trade and the environment', p. 511.

[136] A concept floated by Ernst-Ulrich Petersmann at the Global Environment and Trade
Study (GETS) seminar in Geneva in April 1995.

[137] WTO Committee on Trade and Environment, 'Non-paper by the European Community',
19 February 1996.

If either of the first two routes were chosen, a memorandum of understanding on the interpretation of the GATT would probably be needed. This would set out the criteria which MEA trade provisions would need to satisfy to be considered GATT-compatible, including requirements such as evidence of significant transboundary environmental problems, that trade measures should be proportional to the problem, no more trade-restrictive than necessary, non-discriminatory and transparent, and so on. Effectively, this would remove the right of WTO disputes panels to question aspects of the trade measures, such as their necessity or purpose, while retaining their power to ensure that the measures are applied in accordance with the headnote to Article XX (no disguised protectionism, etc.). Box 4.2 contains two examples of the possible contents of such a memorandum, taken respectively from discussions within the Policy Dialogue on Trade and Environment organized by the US-based Consensus-Building Institute, and from the EU proposals in the WTO.

The behaviour of GATT disputes panels in the two tuna-dolphin cases has given rise to much of the concern about compatibility. As noted above, they have proved increasingly prone to interpret the GATT text in the narrowest possible way, regarding trade impacts as the only matter of concern. A necessary accompaniment of any of the above mechanisms would therefore be an instruction to WTO disputes panels to take other sources of international law – the relevant MEA or MEAs – into account in reaching decisions. In fact, the new WTO disputes settlement procedure means that panels are already more likely to draw on relevant sources of expertise, such as environmental scientists, than their GATT predecessors.

In conclusion, the waiver option is not a particularly satisfactory method of resolution; the waivers would be agreed on an ad hoc basis, time-limited and not predictable in advance (e.g. when an MEA was being negotiated). Amendment of the GATT, in either of the ways described above, is the most definitive and desirable option, firmly entrenching the objective of environmental sustainability (or, at least, the goal of non-conflict with MEAs) at the centre of the international trading regime.

Box 4.2: Reconciling multilateral environmental agreements and GATT

I. From discussions in the Policy Dialogue on Trade and Environment

A measure the principal purpose and effect of which is the protection of the environment, either in the State taking the measure or in a way which contributes to a common interest of human beings, shall be considered compatible with this Agreement if it is reasonable, non-discriminatory and does not restrict trade more than is necessary to promote the purpose of the measure. In considering whether a measure fulfils these requirements, the following may be taken into account, among others:

1   Whether the measure was brought to the attention of the states affected by it or notified to the WTO Secretariat before it was adopted, giving them an adequate opportunity to comment on it.

2   The legislative history of the measure (that is, the reasons why it was proposed, when they are clear).

3   Whether the measure adopted was envisaged or required by a multilateral convention for the conservation of the environment to which the State taking the measure is, or is becoming, a party.

4   Whether the restriction on trade is the principal element in the measure, or is merely one of a number of provisions for conservation of the environment. (A measure is more likely to be genuinely for environmental purposes if it is part of broader environmental or technical or financial assistance legislation.)

5   The extent and the likelihood of the damage to the environment which the measure is intended to avoid or reduce, which may be assessed on the basis of the precautionary principle, in the light of the evidence available.

6   The extent of the contribution which the measure is likely to make to reducing or avoiding that damage.

7   The extent of the adverse effects on trade which will result from the measure.

8   Whether the measure has particularly serious effects on the exports of one or more countries and, if so, whether all reasonable measures have been taken to avoid, reduce or offset these effects.

9   The extent of the adverse consequences, if any, of the measure within the State adopting the measure (such consequences show that the State taking the measure is also making sacrifices).

10 Whether the effectiveness of a scientifically based international environmental or conservation standard is being diminished.

II. From proposals put forward by the EU for discussion in the WTO

1 For the purpose of this Understanding, an MEA is an international written instrument, adopted in conformity with the customary international law as codified by the Vienna Convention on the Law of Treaties, creating legal obligations among parties and aimed at solving environmental problems the solution of which requires action at the international level.

2 *(Option 1)* Subject to the requirements of the headnote to Article XX, measures taken pursuant to specific provisions of an MEA shall be presumed to be 'necessary' for the achievement of the environmental objectives of the MEA *if the MEA in question:*

(Option 2) Subject to the requirements of the headnote to Article XX, measures taken pursuant to specific provisions of an MEA shall be presumed to be 'necessary' for the protection of the environment *if the MEA in question:*

   (a) is open to participation by all parties concerned about the environmental objectives of the agreement;
   (b) reflects, through adequate participation, the interests of parties concerned, including parties with relevant significant trade and economic interests.

3 MEA Secretariats should be requested to inform the WTO Secretariat of any provisions within an MEA which envisage the use of trade measures. Trade measures taken pursuant to an MEA remain subject to the transparency requirements under existing WTO Agreements.

Dispute settlement

4 In the event of a panel being established in response to a complaint against a trade measure taken pursuant to specific provisions of an MEA, the Panel shall review whether the MEA satisfies the criteria of this Understanding.

5 *(Option 1)* Measures taken pursuant to specific provisions of an MEA complying with the provisions of this Understanding shall be deemed to be necessary to achieve the environmental objectives of the MEA but shall remain subject to the requirements of the headnote to Article XX.
   (Option 2) Measures taken pursuant to specific provisions of an MEA complying with the provisions of this Understanding shall be deemed to be necessary to protect the environment but shall remain subject to the requirements of the headnote to Article XX.

6 The possibility to request technical expertise, as foreseen by Article 13 of the Dispute Settlement Understanding, should be seized by a Panel called to judge on the legality of a trade measure taken pursuant to an MEA, if necessary through consultation with the Secretariat of the MEA in question.

Chapter 5

Developing countries and the Montreal Protocol

The thrust towards trade liberalization promoted by the GATT and the WTO is founded on the economic theory of comparative advantage. It is often asserted that the theory leads to the conclusion that free trade is superior to no trade, or even that some trade is superior to no trade, for all countries in all circumstances.[138] In fact, it does nothing of the sort, and moves towards trade liberalization generally result in a complex outcome involving winners and losers. As one of the architects of trade theory, Paul Samuelson, remarked: 'Practical men and economic theorists have always known that trade may help some people and hurt others.'[139] In theory, the losers can be compensated by the winners through resource transfers paid for from the gains from trade – but in practice there is no real mechanism to ensure this happens, which may help to explain the rapid postwar growth in income differentials both between countries and within them.

Nevertheless, there is no evidence to suggest that the situation is improved by the erection of additional trade barriers, which is why trade economists, and developing countries, tend to view with suspicion trade restrictions erected for environmental reasons. But in the case of the Montreal Protocol, there *is* in effect an international compensatory mechanism designed to transfer resources to the 'losers': the Multilateral Fund.[140] As we saw in Chapter 3, it was the combination of the Fund and the trade restrictions directed against non-parties – the 'carrots' together with the 'sticks' – which was so effective in persuading so many developing countries to accede to the treaty.

---

[138] See Paul Ekins, *Trading Off the Future: Making World Trade Environmentally Sustainable* (London: New Economics Foundation, 1993), for a full discussion of this argument.

[139] Cited in ibid., p. 2.

[140] Though this is not, of course, its formal purpose, which is to share the burden of the incremental costs of ODS phase-out.

Chapter 2 describes the structure and operation of the Multilateral Fund. In this chapter we examine the available information on the impact of the trade restrictions of the Protocol on developing countries, the extent to which they may be offset by the use of the Fund, and a number of specific trade issues which have arisen within the ozone regime.

5.1 Trade and competitiveness

UNCTAD studies on the trade and competitiveness effects of the Montreal Protocol show that developing countries seem to have been affected more significantly than developed countries, though outcomes vary substantially depending on particular circumstances.[141]

In some sectors (particularly refrigeration and air-conditioning), substitute chemicals have proved more expensive than the original CFCs (and CFC prices may rise as production falls towards phase-out), raising developing countries' industrial costs if they purchase from industrialized country producers. Poland, for example, which possesses no ODS production facilities, found that the costs of polyurethane for upholstering furniture rose substantially. This would particularly affect international competitiveness if the products affected were exported. Studies in Poland and Colombia showed expected impacts on sectors using refrigeration: flowers, fruit, vegetables and processed meat.

Exports of products containing ODS may similarly become less competitive if demand falls in the importing countries. Restrictions in non-Article 5 countries, such as excise taxes or labelling requirements, have acted to depress demand. Furthermore, many transnational companies now simply refuse to purchase products containing CFCs, and an increasingly large number of customers are unenthusiastic about acquiring goods and equipment which may be unserviceable in the foreseeable future. China, for example, found that its export trade in refrigerators fell by 58%

---

[141] UNCTAD, *Effects of Environmental Policies, Standards and Regulations on Market Access and Competitiveness,* 28 March 1995 (TD/B/WG.6/6); UNCTAD, *Environment, International Competitiveness and Development: Lessons from Empirical Studies: The Policy Debate on Trade, Environment and Development,* 12 September 1995 (TD/B/WG.6/10). Note that these studies provide indicative rather than quantitative evidence.

between 1988 and 1991, and similar declines were experienced in ODS-containing products.[142] Firms which had been able to switch to other free technology, on the other hand, increased exports. (This helped to persuade China to move faster than required to phase out Annex A and B substances, adopting a phase-out target date of 2005, five years earlier than necessary; see Chapter 2.) Growers in Zimbabwe, where methyl bromide is used in horticulture as well as in bulk grain storage, are concerned about falling demand for exports as industrialized countries apply controls to the chemical.

Studies in Malaysia, however, reveal little or no effect on the refrigeration and air-conditioning industry, perhaps because the country has always been at the cutting edge of technological development in these sectors; production and exports have increased strongly. Unit prices have risen along with raw material costs, suggesting that higher production costs have been successfully passed on to customers, and/or that productivity has risen. In fact, developing country exports to OECD countries of some products which could contain ODS (trade statistics do not distinguish) – such as refrigerators and freezing equipment – have been growing much more rapidly than intra-OECD trade in such products.

Competitiveness may also be adversely affected by the costs of converting production lines and technologies which use ODS, or the rising costs and difficulties of servicing with ODS in the process of phase-out. This is, of course, the problem which the Multilateral Fund was designed to counter, but experience shows that access to such financial support is uneven. Large firms in general enjoy better access than smaller enterprises. Also, there is the question of adequacy of funding; the incremental costs of conversion for India, for example, were estimated by the Indian government at $1.4–2.4 billion, about four times the size of the entire Multilateral Fund for the period 1993–5. This is almost certainly, however, a substantial overestimate, probably assuming that alternative technologies and ODS are always more expensive, which has not been the general experience; World Bank estimates of the costs of Indian conversion are $320–482 million.[143] However, some developing countries do face diffi-

---

[142] UNEP, *1994 Report of the Economic Options Committee*, p. 6-10.
[143] See also the discussion concerning Korea in Chapter 3.

culties in obtaining the appropriate technology; OECD-produced equipment, for example, is rarely tested in tropical conditions.

Competitiveness arguments can cut both ways. Multilateral Fund support for conversion effectively means that developing country enterprises are being subsidized to compete with ODS producers and consumers in the developed world.[144] Although this is inevitable and in most cases desirable, if it is so effective as to drive industrialized country companies out of a particular market completely, even if their costs are lower and productivity higher, this may represent an economically sub-optimal outcome.

5.2 'Basic domestic needs' and exports

Some of the competitiveness problems anticipated by developing countries could be offset in either or both of two ways. First, domestic production of ODS which are being phased out in non-Article 5 countries could be increased. As described in Chapter 2, a developing country with an annual level of consumption of Annex A ODS of less than 0.3 kg per capita is entitled to delay for ten years its compliance with the control measures for Annex A and B ODS 'in order to meet its basic domestic needs'.[145] Second, non-Article 5 countries could continue production of CFCs (after domestic phase-out) for export to Article 5 countries. The former are entitled to exceed their production limit by 10% (during phase-out) or 15% (after phase-out) of their 1986 (Annex A), 1989 (Annex B) or 1991 (Annex E) production in order to meet these needs of Article 5 countries.[146]

The question of the availability of ODS for such 'basic domestic needs' has proved a matter of some concern to Article 5 parties, as it was not at

---

[144] Multilateral Fund support for projects which benefit enterprises that export part of their production to non-Article 5 countries is in fact limited, depending on the proportion of production that is exported – if this is greater than 70%, for example, no support is permissible. See *Report of the Executive Committee to the Seventh Meeting of the Parties,* 25 November 1995 (UNEP/OzL.Pro.7/7), p. 10.

[145] Montreal Protocol, Article 5.1.

[146] An interesting question arises in the case of Taiwan, which appears to be intending to continue to produce CFCs for export after phase-out, even though it was *not* a producer in 1986. It is of course not a signatory of the Montreal Protocol, though so far has adhered strictly to its provisions to avoid being treated as a non-party.

all clear that the industrialized world's ODS producers would want to maintain production for this purpose after their major markets in developed countries had disappeared, and as domestic production in Article 5 countries is still relatively limited. The matter was considered at the 1992 Copenhagen Meeting of the Parties,[147] and again at the 1995 Vienna Meeting.

The TEAP investigated the question of supplies of CFCs, halons, carbon tetrachloride and methyl chloroform to Article 5 parties.[148] The data suggested that in 1996, Article 5 producers would supply about 45% of all Article 5 countries' consumption of these four categories of ODS. Non-Article 5 producers would then have to export a total of about 115,000 tonnes to meet the remaining needs, which represents only about 40% of their allowable production after phase-out in their home markets. In fact, installed capacity in Article 5 countries is so much higher than production that probably all their consumption needs could be met by their own producers, with the exception of halons and methyl chloroform – assuming that Article 5 countries are able to trade freely between themselves. Possible further shortfalls of carbon tetrachloride and CFC-113, -114 and -115 could appear in future years if domestic production did not expand. Alternatively, allowable production in non-Article 5 countries would be sufficient by itself to meet the needs of Article 5 countries in all categories, with the probable exception of some halons. There seemed little danger, the TEAP concluded, of absolute supply shortages (see Table 5.1).

The TEAP, however, identified a number of other factors. Unanticipated high growth in demand for controlled substances could lead to higher prices and possible shortages. A falling number of producers could lead to monopoly pricing. Illegal markets in non-Article 5 countries could divert supplies from Article 5 states, and also undercut legitimate producers so severely as to drive them out of the Article 5 market, particularly as they face small production runs and diminishing prospects. On the other hand, Article 5 countries were already facing diminishing export opportunities not only for ODS but for products containing ODS (see section 5.1 above).

---

[147] Decision IV/29 of the Parties to the Montreal Protocol.
[148] *Technology and Economic Assessment Panel: Report to the Parties, November 1995* (Nairobi: UNEP, 1995), Part IV.

Table 5.1: Estimates of world-wide supply potential and consumption in Article 5 countries, 1996

	Allowable production in non-Article 5 countries[a]	Maximum allowable production in Article 5 countries[b]	Maximum allowable production in Article 5 plus non-Article 5 countries	Estimated consumption in Article 5 countries
AI	151,811[c]	149,388	301,199	149,388
AII	5,939[c]	8,350	14,289	10,726
BII[d]	30,382	6,400	36,782	5,270
BIII	98,391	4,600	102,991	38,200

Units: tonnes.

[a] 'Allowable' production by non-Article 5 countries is defined as the 15% of their 1986 baseline production allowed by the Protocol to meet the basic domestic needs of the Article 5 countries during the phase-out and grace periods.

[b] Maximum 'allowable' production by the Article 5 countries is installed production capacity that would be usable under the control measures of the Protocol. In the case of CFCs for 1996, it is assumed that maximum allowable production by Article 5 countries will be equal to their estimated consumption.

[c] Production of halons 1211 and 1301 has ceased in non-Article 5 countries. As a result, this quantity is not available to meet the domestic needs of Article 5 countries. However, recycled halons are available on the world market, and these can be purchased by Article 5 countries to meet their needs.

[d] The estimates in the table do not take into account data on carbon tetrachloride for feedstock and process agent use.

Source: UNEP, *Technology and Economic Assessment Panel: Report to the Parties, November 1995*, Part IV.

The TEAP concluded that phase-out of Annex A and B ODS in Article 5 countries, assisted by the Multilateral Fund, would help reduce dependence on controlled substances, and measures such as import taxes could help to avoid problems associated with under-priced illegal imports.

The question of trade *between* Article 5 countries, however, gave rise to considerable dispute between the parties to the Protocol. At the first Meeting of the Parties after the agreement was negotiated, the question was raised whether production for 'basic domestic needs' in Article 5 countries allowed for the possibility of export. The general opinion among the original negotiators was that the phrase 'basic domestic needs' was intended to refer only to production for domestic use, and could not be extended to exports,[149] with the possible exception of countries which were already exporting.[150] Developing countries, however – particularly India and China – argued that the expansion of exports was itself a 'basic domestic need' of a developing economy, and that ODS exports should therefore be permitted. Furthermore, as the TEAP report commented, the 'strict interpretation of basic domestic needs would segment the world market in a way that would reduce choice for users and lead to inefficient markets by reducing competition'.[151]

The problem arises because the term was never defined in the original agreement. The first Meeting of the Parties failed to resolve the matter, deciding only that: '"Basic domestic needs" referred to in Articles 2 and 5 of the Protocol should be understood as not to allow production of products containing controlled substances to expand for the purpose of supplying other countries.'[152] The issue of exports of the ODS themselves was not resolved at the time, but subsequently became a much bigger issue. Indian producers in particular have recently been aggressively expanding production and exports to other Article 5 countries – 'to prevent the premature death of our [manufacturing] plants,' stated Rabinder Kaul of India's Refrigerator Gas Manufacturers Association in July 1995. 'During the last few years, we have established a marketing network in 30 countries which I think is threatening them [the West].'[153] The argument was presented in terms of a Western attempt to prevent Third World industrialization. Indian production of CFCs reported to the Ozone Secretariat grew by 419% between 1986 and 1993 and in 1993 exceeded consumption by over 6,000 tonnes.[154]

The 1994 Meeting of the Parties requested the Open-Ended Working Group to examine the issue and make recommendations to the 1995

[149] James A. Losey (formerly US EPA) and Patrick Széll (Department of the Environment), personal communications.

[150] G. Victor Buxton (Environment Canada), personal communication.

[151] UNEP, *Technology and Economic Assessment Panel: Report to the Parties, November 1995*, p. IV-6.

[152] Decision I/12C of the Parties to the Montreal Protocol.

[153] Cited in Jim Vallette, *Deadly Complacency: US CFC Production, the Black Market, and Ozone Depletion* (Washington, DC: Ozone Action, 1995), p. 12.

[154] UNEP, *Report of the Secretariat to the Seventh Meeting of the Parties to the Montreal Protocol*, 25 September 1995 (UNEP/OzL.Pro.7/6).

Meeting. Members of the OECD group of parties argued for tight restrictions on such exports as they were undermining global efforts at phase-out. They tabled an amendment to the Protocol aiming to limit exports of controlled substances from Article 5 countries to situations where a Meeting of the Parties determined that there would otherwise be a shortfall in supply, and where production utilized only existing capacity and did not exceed 10% or 15% of the 1994 production level. India tabled a counter-amendment removing all constraints on trade in ODS between Article 5 countries. The ensuing arguments between OECD and developing country groups formed one of the more acrimonious sessions at the Open-Ended Working Group in August–September 1995.

Compromise was reached in Vienna three months later.[155] The parties recognized the needs of Article 5 countries for 'adequate and quality supplies of ODS at fair and equitable prices' and the need to avoid monopolies of supply. Article 5 producers were free from any restraints on export of Annex A and B ODS to other Article 5 consumers until the first control measure came into force, i.e. for CFCs on 1 July 1999. After that date, exports would be allowed only within the production limits set by the Protocol. Parties were called upon to monitor and regulate this trade through the issue of import and export licences, and to report full data to the Ozone Secretariat. From 7 December 1995, however (the date of adoption of the decision), no party should install or commission any new production capacity for Annex A or B ODS. The proposed licensing system, including a ban on unlicensed imports and exports, was to be incorporated into the Protocol by the ninth Meeting of the Parties, in 1997, and consideration was to be given to permitting trade in ODS only where parties were in full compliance with the provisions of the treaty, including its data reporting requirements (which, since the majority of parties are usually late in reporting data, would have a wide impact). The parties were also to consider whether to extend these proposed mechanisms to all other ODS covered by the Protocol.

---

[155] Decision VII/9 of the Parties to the Montreal Protocol.

5.3 'Technology dumping'

A rather less contentious matter has also arisen in respect of developing countries, namely the question of 'technology dumping'. The issue was raised during 1995 by Mauritius. A hotel chain had removed air-conditioning equipment from its hotels in an industrialized country, as it used refrigerants which were about to become unobtainable there (as they were due for phase-out on 1 January 1996), and installed it in hotels belonging to the same chain in Mauritius. It became clear during later discussions that this was a matter of widespread concern to many developing countries, which had no desire to see their efforts to implement accelerated phase-out schedules undermined by the movement of obsolete technology. South Africa announced that it was considering regulations banning both the import of products containing CFCs and the export of equipment designed to run on CFCs. Anecdotal evidence from Kenya suggested that second-hand CFC-using refrigerators from European countries such as Germany or Sweden (where markets for hydrocarbon-using fridges have expanded rapidly) were being imported and sold at very low prices (e.g. £40). Even worse, it was suggested that some second-hand equipment from Europe was being illicitly shipped to developing countries by firms paid to break it up and dispose of the refrigerants safely.

Suspicions were raised that some suppliers in non-Article 5 countries were deliberately encouraging such 'technology dumping' as a means of maintaining markets. The non-Article 5 countries themselves, however, have no desire to see developments which might lead to extra drains on Multilateral Fund resources; and at least some Article 5 countries have deliberately acquired obsolete technology from non-Article 5 producers for ODS production.[156] The 1995 Meeting of the Parties accordingly resolved to recommend parties 'to take legislative and administrative measures, including labelling of products, to regulate the export and import, as appropriate, of products containing substances listed in Annexes A and B of the Protocol and of technology used in the manufacturing of such products'.[157] A number of parties suggested a 'prior informed consent'

---

[156] For example, India's purchase of a CFC-12 production plant from Allied Chemical in 1988: see Chapter 3.
[157] Decision VII/32 of the Parties to the Montreal Protocol.

procedure of the kind increasingly used, for example, for shipments of hazardous chemicals, through which both exporter and importer must give written permission for the trade in advance.[158]

(At the Open-Ended Working Group in May 1995, when the draft decision was under consideration, the parties decided to consult with the WTO to ensure that any such restrictions on trade conformed with the provisions of the GATT; a WTO observer was present at the following meeting in August–September. She was not notably forthcoming, circulating a statement only to the effect that the WTO Secretariat possessed no authority to interpret the GATT and had referred the request to the WTO Committee on Trade and Environment; she requested clarification of precisely what trade measures were contemplated and how any disputes between parties would be resolved. This did not go down particularly well at the time, sparking off a discussion about whether the parties really wished to refer anything at all to the WTO, with the view expressed that it was up to the parties to the Montreal Protocol, not to WTO members, to develop and apply the ozone regime – an illustration, in many ways, of the differences in approach between trade and environment negotiators. The WTO Committee consultations had not been completed by the time of the Vienna Meeting.)

A complete ban on the trade (effectively an extension of the ban on imports of goods listed in Annex D of the Protocol from non-parties to all parties) would be feasible (though probably difficult to enforce) but clearly undesirable in cases where the goods themselves are welcome. Few developing countries are manufacturers of such goods, and thus must import them from somewhere; permitting them only to import goods containing ODS replacements negates the value of the delay in phase-out. The problem is essentially caused by some developing countries wishing to accelerate the phase-out schedules, which in itself is clearly a desirable goal.

5.4 Conclusion

All these issues underline the relationship between the restrictions on trade and the provision of financial support through the Multilateral Fund: the

---

[158] See UNEP, *Report of the Executive Director to the Seventh Meeting of the Parties to the Montreal Protocol*, 6 November 1995 (UNEP/OzL.Pro.7/3/Add.1).

'sticks' and the 'carrots'. As noted above, it is this combination of features that has been so important in persuading so many developing countries to join the Montreal Protocol, thereby rendering its implementation more effective. In principle, and given adequate funding, there seems no reason why the mechanisms of the Multilateral Fund should not be able to compensate developing countries for the negative impacts on competitiveness which some of them have suffered as a result of the implementation of the Protocol. In effect, this is what the Fund is doing, through its support for the incremental costs of phase-out.

The ten-year delay in compliance to which Article 5 countries are entitled, however, has led to problems and anomalies, particularly for individual countries aiming to move faster than the phase-out schedules; in retrospect it might have been preferable to have specified a shorter delay, such as the five years that was initially contemplated during the original negotiations. However, trade flows between developing and industrialized countries create a dynamic for precisely this phase-out. It is interesting that the solution to many of these problems is seen in closer monitoring of, and possibly further restrictions on, trade in ODS and products containing ODS.

Future MEAs, therefore, need to consider the implications of differential phase-outs, and to define carefully terms such as 'basic domestic needs' and the conditions under which permitted trade should be carried out. It seems likely, furthermore, that the provision of additional financial support for new control measures (due to be discussed in 1996) would, by encouraging faster phase-out, assist in resolving the anomalies highlighted in this chapter. It would also help in tackling some of the new implementation problems faced by the ozone regime, the subject to which we turn in the next chapter.

Chapter 6

New problems for the ozone regime

As the Montreal Protocol regime has evolved and grown more complex since 1987, developments have occurred which have not, by and large, been foreseen – though, arguably, some of them should have been. This chapter examines two areas of particular concern in respect of the international trade in ODS.

6.1 Non-compliance

Non-compliance with the reporting provisions of the Montreal Protocol has been a problem for several years; data have frequently been submitted late or in an incomplete form, or not submitted at all. The situation improved after July 1994, when the Implementation Committee adopted the practice of inviting offending parties to appear before it to explain non-compliance.[159] More serious problems have arisen, however, in the cases of a number of the countries of central and eastern Europe and the former Soviet Union, or 'countries with economies in transition' (CEITs).

The massive geopolitical and economic changes taking place in the CEITs have thrown up a complex set of interrelated problems. The nine states which existed when the Montreal Protocol was negotiated, which apart from Albania all became signatories, have now dissolved into 27, of which 18 are signatories; of these, five are currently classified as Article 5 countries, and several of the non-signatories would probably be eligible for Article 5 status (see Table 6.1). With the dissolution of the Soviet Union, the official reporting of production and consumption data by the largest consumer and only producer in the region ceased; many of its successor

---

[159] Owen Greene, 'Emerging challenges for the Montreal Protocol', *The Globe* 27, October 1995.

Table 6.1: Countries with economies in transition and their status under the Montreal Protocol

Signatories	Non-signatories[a]
Non-Article 5	
Belarus, Bulgaria, Czech Republic, Hungary, Latvia, Lithuania, Poland, Russia, Slovakia, Slovenia, Turkmenistan, Ukraine, Uzbekistan	Armenia, Azerbaijan, Estonia, Georgia,[c] Kazakhstan, Kyrgyzstan, Moldova, Tajikistan
Article 5	
Bosnia,[b] Croatia, Macedonia,[b] Romania, Serbia/Montenegro	Albania

[a] The categorization of non-signatories for Article 5 status is an estimate, since in general full data are lacking from these countries. Categorization also depends on UN definition as a 'developing country'; successor states to the former Soviet Union are not so defined, as the USSR itself was not a developing country. However, the ODS consumption of all of the countries listed in the non-Article 5, non-signatory cell here is currently estimated to fall below the 0.3 kg per capita threshold, so categorization as a 'developing country' would render them eligible for Article 5 status. Yugoslavia was categorized as an Article 5 country, and so are its successor states, with the exception of Slovenia, which has been re-categorized.

[b] Temporarily categorized as Article 5, pending receipt of complete data.

[c] Georgia announced at the Vienna Meeting of the Parties that it had acceded to the Protocol, but this has not yet been formally reported.

Source: UNEP, *Assessment of Basic Problems Confronting Countries with Economies in Transition in Complying with the Montreal Protocol: Report of the TEAP Ad-Hoc Working Group on CEIT Aspects,* November 1995.

states have experienced difficulty in collecting and reporting adequate data. Furthermore, it rapidly became clear that many of them were unlikely to comply either with the phase-out obligations of the Montreal Protocol or with their contribution requirements to the Multilateral Fund, as a result of political and economic disruption and the generally low priority given to environmental policy as a result. As the Russian environment minister pointed out in his speech to the Vienna Meeting of the Parties in December 1995, his country was now significantly poorer than a number of the Article 5 countries it was supposed to help.

In May 1995, the Russian Prime Minister, Viktor Chernomyrdin, submitted a statement to the parties which admitted that, while the Russian

Federation remained committed to the fulfilment of the terms of the agreement, full compliance with the phase-out target of 1996 would be impossible. He estimated that by 1997 consumption of ODS would have fallen by about 85% of 1990 levels,[160] and formally requested a four-year deferment of the time limit (to 2000) for the production and consumption of CFCs, carbon tetrachloride and methyl chloroform, and a three-year deferment of the time limit (to 1997) for the production and consumption of halons. A similar statement was issued at the Open-Ended Working Group meeting in August–September 1995, signed by Belarus, Bulgaria and Ukraine, as well as the Russian Federation, and Armenia, Georgia and Kyrgyzstan as non-members who intended soon to accede. The Russian government also indicated that without additional financial support from the GEF (as a non-Article 5 country, Russia is not eligible for assistance from the Multilateral Fund), complete phase-out would probably not be feasible even by these target dates. Conversion costs of $600 million were later estimated by the Russian Ministry of Environment,[161] though a TEAP estimate was much lower, putting total costs for all CEITs at about $265 million. The Russian Federation added that it intended to impose a requirement for licences for exports and imports of ODS to and from other Montreal Protocol parties from January 1996, border controls between the former Soviet republics having been entirely lacking previously.

An ad hoc working group under the TEAP was formed in late 1994 to establish reliable sources of data and investigate the issues; it reported in November 1995.[162] The group accepted that most non-Article 5 CEITs were likely to experience short periods of non-compliance over the next three to five years, with the biggest problems arising in the former Soviet republics. The centrally planned nature of the former Soviet economy, and

---

[160] The Russian consumption figure for 1990 was estimated as equivalent to the pro rata share of Soviet consumption in 1986, the official baseline figure, though there are severe doubts about the accuracy of all data reported from the region.

[161] *Global Environmental Change Report* VII:23, 8 December 1995, p. 1.

[162] UNEP, *Assessment of Basic Problems Confronting Countries with Economies in Transition in Complying with the Montreal Protocol: Report of the TEAP Ad-Hoc Working Group on CEIT Aspects,* November 1995.

the resulting interdependence of the economies of its successor states, made the problem quite complex. The imposition of the trade barriers with non-parties required by the Protocol (and Protocol signatories trading with non-parties could be considered themselves to be in non-compliance, and therefore non-parties) would have profound implications. Russia was the main supplier of ODS to almost all of the other CEITs, and many of them exported products containing ODS back to Russia, as well as to each other; in Soviet days, factories in Latvia and Lithuania, for example, had satisfied most of the aerosol demand for the USSR as a whole. The possibilities of some countries reopening mothballed ODS production facilities (such as the Tajik plant in Yavan, capable of producing up to 30,000 tonnes per year) and of increasing reliance on black market supplies obviously had to be avoided if possible. There was a strong case, the TEAP group concluded, for treating the region as a whole in taking decisions on the consequences of non-compliance by some countries, and on the availability of funding and technical support. The group outlined a range of options, most of which accepted the principle of phase-out extension, but specifically criticized the Russian Federation for continuing failure to comply with the reporting obligations.

The Implementation Committee of the Montreal Protocol is responsible for dealing with cases of non-compliance and reporting back to the Meeting of the Parties with recommendations. The non-compliance procedure, agreed in full in 1992 (see Chapter 2), is designed to give maximum opportunities for compliance as opposed to punishment; the indicative list of measures that can be taken includes technical and financial assistance, followed by the issuing of cautions, followed by suspension. In this last case, the country concerned would become effectively a non-party to the Protocol, thus becoming subject to the trade restrictions as well as losing access to financial support and the decision-making procedure. There never having been a case of non-compliance before the emergence of the CEITs problem (other than those connected with late reporting of data), however, it was entirely unclear how the procedure would work in practice, and it was hoped that such relatively drastic measures would never need to be taken.[163]

---

[163] Hugo Schally (Implementation Committee), personal communication.

The Committee considered the position throughout the second half of 1995. As well as urging CEITs not party to the Protocol to accede or provide data demonstrating compliance – partly in order to avoid parties trading in ODS with them to be considered to be in non-compliance[164] – it prepared draft decisions for the Vienna Meeting relating to five CEITs.[165] In the cases of Poland and Bulgaria,[166] the Committee recognized that both countries were in compliance for 1995 but that there were possibilities of non-compliance the following year; in each case, the Committee would revert to consideration of the options if necessary. Belarus and Ukraine,[167] where non-compliance in 1996 was believed more likely, were treated at more length. The two countries agreed to provide detailed information on their ODS phase-out programmes. They undertook not to export any virgin, recycled or recovered substance controlled under the Protocol to any non-Article 5 party other than members of the Commonwealth of Independent States (i.e. the former Soviet republics apart from the three Baltic states). Although neither was a producer of ODS, this would control any trans-shipment. On the basis of these agreements, the Committee recommended financial assistance for phase-out programmes, under close supervision from the Ozone Secretariat and Implementation Committee.

The last decision related to the Russian Federation.[168] While recognizing that the country was in compliance with its obligations in 1995, the Committee expected a situation of non-compliance in 1996. Russia was required to submit the same types of information as were required of Belarus and Ukraine, but with a specific undertaking to submit more detailed information by the end of January 1996. The country was also to accept the trade restrictions (i.e. no exports to non-CIS industrialized

---

[164] *Report of the Implementation Committee under the Non-Compliance Procedure for the Montreal Protocol on the Work of its Tenth Meeting,* 30 August 1995 (UNEP/OzL.Pro/ ImpCom/10/4), para. 39.

[165] For a full discussion of the work of the Implementation Committee on these matters, see Owen Greene, 'The Montreal Protocol: implementation and development in 1995', in J. Poole and R. Guthrie (eds), *Verification 1996: Arms Control, Environment and Peacekeeping* (Boulder and London: Westview Press, forthcoming, 1996).

[166] Decisions VII/15 and VII/16 of the Parties to the Montreal Protocol.

[167] Decisions VII/17 and VII/19 of the Parties to the Montreal Protocol.

[168] Decision VII/18 of the Parties to the Montreal Protocol.

countries). On the basis of these agreements, financial and technical support would be considered.

The Russian delegation at Vienna made its objections to the last two elements of this decision clear throughout the meeting, believing that the Committee had failed to take sufficient account of the economic and political turmoil its country was suffering, and that the application of these measures was tantamount to imposing sanctions against a party that was still fully in compliance with the treaty – that is, in effect, a revision of the Protocol. If the recommendations were accepted, warned the Russian environment minister, 'the process of replacing ODS will significantly lose momentum and will become worse by being controlled, measures to strengthen export controls will not be taken, there will be a trend towards illegal production of ODS by producers and the use of these products by consumers. There will be another incentive (over and above those already existing) for autarky, which will be deliberately exploited by the corresponding political forces.'

Despite these dire warnings, not a single country expressed support for the Russian reservations; although it is possible to sympathize with the Russian request to be allowed to continue producing Annex A and B ODS for domestic consumption, it is rather more difficult to justify production for export. On the contrary, a developing country lobby, led by Venezuela (a CFC producer), argued for *strengthening* the trade restrictions by banning Russian exports to Article 5 countries; trade was to be permitted only with non-Article 5 CIS members, and re-export from those countries was also to be banned.[169] At the last session of the meeting, the Russian delegation denounced these provisions, stated that the Federation retained its right to consider all circumstances and draw the corresponding conclusions with regard to further compliance, and left the hall. As of late February 1996, Russia had still not submitted the data required of it. The ozone regime is thus now faced with its first case of serious and persistent non-compliance. Among other outcomes, this will eliminate, or at least

---

[169] The eventual wording of the decision, however, while specifically permitting exports to non-Article 5 CIS members, is silent on exports to Article 5 parties, whether CIS members or not; its impact is therefore unclear. The EU currently permits imports of Russian ODS if intended for re-export to Article 5 countries.

delay, the provision of funding from the GEF, which in turn will probably mean that Russia will not implement its own ODS reduction programme, which was reliant on GEF assistance.[170]

6.2 Illegal trade

This new problem of Russian non-compliance feeds directly into the second major problem threatening the ozone regime: the matter of illegal trade in ODS. A significant proportion of Russian production currently appears to be entering other markets illegally. Although this is a trade issue, it has little to do with the trade provisions of the Montreal Protocol, arising primarily from the treaty's control measures. The problem is most acute – and has so far been most effectively addressed – in the US, although there is evidence of a black market and a 'grey' market (in virgin material disguised as, or blended with, recycled substances) in the EU and in Asia as well. Chemical industry sources estimated in late 1995 that up to 20% of CFCs then in use across the world were bought on the black market.[171]

Illegal trade in the US

The US has experienced more acute problems for two reasons. First, 90% of US automobiles are fitted with mobile air-conditioning systems (MACS), compared to about 10% of European vehicles (though this proportion is increasing). This leads not only to a larger demand for refrigerant fluids – from a sector which has experienced difficulty and high costs in converting out of CFCs – but also to a network of small users (garages servicing and repairing cars) among whom legislation controlling ODS is more difficult to promote, monitor and enforce. An estimated 100 million US autos are fitted with MACS which cannot be adapted for CFC substitutes, but must be retrofitted with new equipment at costs typically of $200–300 per vehicle, but ranging up to $800.[172] Second, the US introduction in 1990 of a CFC excise tax at the point of sale or first use has

---

[170] *Global Environmental Change Report* VIII:4, 23 February 1996, p. 3.

[171] *The Economist,* 9 December 1995, p. 89.

[172] CNN-TV news story, 19 January 1995.

created a substantial incentive for tax avoidance. The value of the tax – $3.35 per pound of CFC-12 in 1993, rising to $5.35 in 1995 and $5.80 in 1996, and increasing by $0.45 per year until 2000 – now substantially exceeds the retail price of about $2 per pound. (A floor stocks tax of $1 per pound was applied from 1 January 1995, for holdings of more than 400 pounds, to discourage hoarding of CFCs purchased at the lower price in 1994. An additional $0.45 per pound will similarly be applied in each successive year.) One of the first indications of the extent of the black market was the failure of CFC prices quoted to retailers to rise in line with these excise tax increases.

This combination of circumstances has resulted in a black market in CFCs in the US variously estimated at between 20 and 40 million pounds a year (about 9,000–18,000 tonnes) – worth between $150 and $300 million at legitimate prices.[173] If even the lower figure was accurate in 1994, it represented about 20% of all virgin CFC-12 imported into the US in that year.[174] If the volume of smuggled material remains significant after the CFC phase-out on 1 January 1996, it will clearly threaten the integrity of the ozone regime, and hence the recovery of the ozone layer.

In response to persistent pressure from the fluorocarbons industry, alarmed at seeing its legitimate products undercut, on 25 October 1994 the US government announced the establishment of an inter-agency task force, involving the Environmental Protection Agency (EPA), Customs Service, Internal Revenue Service (IRS) and the Departments of Commerce and Justice. The EPA is responsible for the issuing of consumption allowances, specifying on an annual basis the quantities of ODS which can be manufactured and imported for consumption in the US; the total volume has been reduced each year (to zero in 1996) in pursuit of eventual phase-out. Training and education, particularly of customs officers, has helped to raise the profile of the issue and to improve enforcement. Customs investigations, codenamed 'Operation Cool Breeze', concentrated resources on tracking imports, ensuring that licences for import or trans-shipment were present and genuine. The IRS has expended effort

---

[173] Tom Land (EPA), personal communication; *Financial Times,* survey of the chemicals industry, 27 October 1995, p. 4; Vallette, *Deadly Complacency,* p. 16.
[174] *Global Environmental Change Report* VI:21, 11 November 1994, p. 2.

on companies' tax returns; the value of CFC tax collected in 1994 totalled $1,000 million.[175]

The task force has scored notable successes. One year after its formation, $40 million had been collected in unpaid taxes and penalties, and the IRS estimated that a potential $50 million remained uncollected. By the end of 1995, thirteen individuals had been indicted on counts of smuggling or diverting CFCs into the US, and evading federal excise taxes; ten had been convicted, the first convictions ever for breach of the US Clean Air Act, and 1 million pounds of illegal CFCs impounded.[176] In the most dramatic case, on 29 August 1995 a Ms Irma Henneberg, the manager of a Florida shipping company, was found guilty on 34 charges relating to the false manifesting of cargo to be shipped from Miami. False manifests were filed covering 209 cargo containers, holding almost 4,000 US tons of CFC-12 with a retail value of about $52m. Inspection of the outbound vessels supposedly re-exporting the CFCs from the US (a legal activity) revealed that the cargo containers were not aboard, a conclusion supported by the fact that some of the manifests claimed a greater number of containers per vessel than the ship could actually carry. Since consumption allowances originally issued on the basis of fraudulent documented exports could be considered as unexpended and reissued on the export of the CFCs, the scheme potentially involved substantial further abuse of the system. Each guilty count carried a maximum penalty of five years' imprisonment and a fine of $25,000,[177] but in the end Henneberg was sentenced to a fine of $10,000 and 57 months' imprisonment, together with restrictions on her future employment.[178] In another case, a suspected American CFC smuggler was arrested in Costa Rica, marking the first international extradition effort by the US in respect of a fugitive charged with environmental crimes.[179] In January 1996, a US federal judge handed down the largest

---

[175] *OzonAction* 15, July 1995, p. 7.

[176] Alliance for Responsible Atmospheric Policy (the main US industry coalition) press release, 28 November 1995. The EPA is currently considering what to do with the impounded material; destruction of such a large volume would be highly expensive: Tom Land (EPA), personal communication.

[177] US Department of Justice News Release, 'CFC-12 Conviction', 29 August 1995.

[178] *Global Environmental Change Report* VII:20, 10 November 1995, p. 5.

[179] Ibid., VII:24, 22 December 1995, p. 4.

penalty yet in a conviction for CFC smuggling: 14 months' imprisonment and $3.4 million in tax restitution.[180]

It has been estimated that CFCs are now the second most lucrative commodity smuggled through Miami, exceeded in value only by cocaine. This port experiences a particular problem since it exports legitimately to Article 5 countries in Latin America, providing many opportunities for fraud, as in the Henneberg case, or clandestine re-entry. Canisters of CFCs being illegally re-imported are frequently mislabelled, often as HCFCs or hydrocarbons; sudden increases in requests for licences for imports of these substances can be an indication of illegal activity.[181] In one case, canisters labelled 'Freon' (the DuPont trademark name for CFC-12) were detected in a non-American container. The substance had been produced in the DuPont plant in Mexico, legally sold to a destination in South America and then illegally re-imported into the US in a series of further unregulated transactions.[182]

Another indication of illegal trade is excessive shipments to a particular country. Exports of CFCs from the US to the Dutch Antilles, for example (a territory with a population of about 300,000) reached a total of 1,572 tonnes in 1994, and were estimated at more than 2,000 tonnes for 1995. As US Assistant District Attorney Tom Watts-Fitzgerald commented, this volume of exports to the territory would be 'enough to put a dome over it and cool it until the next century'.[183]

Additional problems have been created by trade in recycled and recovered ODS (see section 3.1). There was some initial confusion in the US over whether the CFC excise tax was payable on imports of recycled or contaminated CFCs, which led to some tax evasion by mistake – or created a convenient excuse. The position was clarified in early 1995, and the EPA instituted a petition process requiring full details and approval of shipments; previously, no allowance system for recycled ODS had been required. The EPA is currently in the process of finalizing a rule requiring similar approval for trans-shipments.[184] More seriously, there is evidence to

---

[180] Ibid., VIII:3, 9 February 1996, p. 5.
[181] Tom Land (EPA), personal communication.
[182] Tony Vogelsberg (DuPont Chemicals), personal communication.
[183] Cited in Vallette, *Deadly Complacency,* p. 16.
[184] Alliance for Responsible Atmospheric Policy press release, 28 November 1995.

suggest that some of the smuggled virgin CFCs is being mislabelled as recycled, or deliberately contaminated to make it appear recycled. After the petition process was instituted, the volume of imports of ODS for recycling fell dramatically, at least among those companies which filed petitions. Canadian attempts to export recycling and recovery equipment to Brazil have proved unsuccessful; it is believed that the easy availability of cheap illegal CFCs had rendered the investment not worthwhile.[185] Whether actually or deliberately contaminated, random samples of suspected illegal CFC-12 in the US have often proved to be far below industry specifications. One sample, for example, had a 50% moisture level and contained ten times the acceptable level of non-absorbable gases, properties which would almost certainly result in serious damage to refrigeration systems.[186]

Illegal trade in Asia

In Asia, Taiwan appears to have experienced the most severe problems. Customs authorities confiscated 20,000 kg of illegal CFCs in 1993 and 40,000 kg in 1994, but estimated that they were catching only about 10% of the smuggled material. The availability of cheap illegal imports is clearly threatening the country's efforts at phase-out, and customs officers are cooperating with the chemicals industry in developing detection techniques. Simple tests include checking the boiling points and pressures of the gases being inspected; dubious cases are referred to industry labs for full analysis. Smuggling techniques are, however, becoming increasingly sophisticated. Nitrogen has been added to cylinders to raise the internal pressure of CFC-12 to what would be expected for HCFC-22, a legal ODS. Another innovation was the fitting of extra jackets containing legal substances round cylinders full of illegal CFCs to mislead customs officers taking samples. Taiwanese actions in retaliation include the planned introduction of new legislation to allow prosecution of the smugglers, and the organization of an international conference on the illegal trade in CFCs during 1996.[187]

---

[185] Friends of the Earth Canada, personal communication.
[186] Alliance for Responsible Atmospheric Policy press release, 27 January 1995.
[187] Johnsee Lee (Association of Ozone Layer Protection in Taiwan) and Jen-Rong Lu (Formosa Plastics Corporation), personal communications.

Illegal trade in Europe

Evidence of smuggling in the European Union is more difficult to come by. The problem seems to be genuinely smaller than in the US because of the relative lack of MACS in European cars, and also because of the general absence of CFC taxes. As a result, however, European customs authorities have been less inclined to take action to investigate and police the black and grey markets which do appear to exist. In March 1995, for instance, DuPont's distributor in Germany was contacted by a firm called META Enterprise Ltd, based in St Petersburg, which offered to make available unspecified (but significant) quantities of 'Freon-12'.[188] In April 1995, a Spanish NGO, CODA, accused two firms, one based in Gibraltar, of importing CFCs from Russia, deliberately adulterating them with water vapour, and selling them to refrigerator and air-conditioner manufacturers.[189] Several months later, the Spanish government admitted the existence of the problem and stepped up border surveillance; one barrier to more direct action appeared to be the lack of sanctions in Spanish legislation against those using banned CFCs.[190]

CFC prices in Europe have not risen as fast as one would expect, given the EU phase-out on 1 January 1995, possibly indicating the existence of illegal supplies; in contrast, the price of R502 (a blend of HCFC-22 and CFC-115), a low-temperature refrigerant not manufactured in Russia, rose rapidly in Britain as stocks expired during 1995.[191] Industry sources estimated that 6,000–10,000 tonnes of CFCs were illegally imported into the EU in 1994.[192] It has been suggested that some of the air-conditioning and refrigeration equipment in the UK is currently serviced by black-market CFCs; one of the big three supermarket chains was reported as having been offered unlimited quantities of CFC-12 for its refrigeration units. If users believe that illegal and cheaper CFCs will be readily available for the

---

[188] Vivian Sheridan (DuPont External Affairs), personal communication.
[189] *Global Environmental Change Report* VII:9, 12 May 1995, p. 3.
[190] Ibid., VII:24, 22 December 1995, p. 7.
[191] Nicholas Schoon, 'Customs inquiry into secret trade in CFCs', *The Independent* 19 September 1995.
[192] Tony Vogelsberg (DuPont Chemicals), personal communication; *Financial Times,* survey of the chemicals industry, 27 October 1995, p. 4.

foreseeable future, this clearly inhibits the development of markets for alternatives.

In December 1995, Eileen Claussen, the leader of the US delegation to the Vienna Meeting, criticized the lack of widespread action against illegal trade outside the US. 'We see no similar efforts elsewhere; in fact, there are some countries where the penalties for the illegal import of CFCs are so small as to be almost laughable, and there is only one enforcement action that has been taken outside the US. This is a situation that is intolerable for the ozone layer.'[193] The only European country which appears to have taken any effective action is the Netherlands, where in 1994 six companies were charged with illegal import and one with illegal export.[194]

Disguising virgin material as recycled is also a problem; users have been offered recycled ODS from Russia, despite the fact that the country is believed to possess no significant recycling facilities.[195] In 1995 the Dutch Environment Inspectorate discovered several dozens of tonnes of virgin CFCs deliberately labelled as recycled.[196]

Goods ostensibly bound for trans-shipment, or inward processing relief (IPR; where imports are processed in some way – sometimes only repackaged – and then re-exported; no duty is payable) have also caused problems. ODS brought in for IPR initially required no import licence, and customs statistics showed substantial volumes entering during 1994. In the face of concern over the possible diversion of imports for IPR into home markets, a licensing system was introduced in January 1995 for monitoring purposes; no limit was set on the volume of licences issued, but proof was required of re-export. (Whether the ultimate destination is legal, of course, is another matter; CFCs entering the US illegally in October and November 1994 had been shipped from Felixstowe.[197]) In 1995, the EU licensed over 12,000 tonnes of CFC imports, of which about 500 tonnes were intended for free circulation, and the remainder for IPR. A far smaller volume of licences has been issued so far in 1996, and the import of ODS

---

[193] Statement of the United States of America to the Vienna Meeting of the Parties, December 1995.

[194] Netherlands CFC Committee, *CFC Action Programme: Annual Report 1994*, p. 31.

[195] Nick Campbell (ICI Klea), personal communication.

[196] Netherlands CFC Committee, *CFC Action Programme: Annual Report 1994*, p. 42.

[197] *Global Environmental Change Report* VII:2, 27 January 1995, p. 3.

from Russia has been restricted to consumption for essential uses and to IPR for re-export to Article 5 countries only.

The production or import of CFCs for chemical feedstock is, of course, legally permitted (see Chapter 2). The definition of 'feedstock', however, appears to have been stretched far beyond its limits by a number of importers, to include the manufacture of expanded polyurethane foams, for example, or the repackaging of CFCs into containers for use in refrigeration.[198] In 1994, the European Commission issued quotas of 16,000 tonnes of CFCs for use as feedstock, whereas the major genuine user in the EU (Zeneca, which uses CFCs as feedstock in the production of pesticides), required only about 1,500 tonnes.[199]

In response to these concerns, a working group was established by the European Commission in 1995, comprising representatives of industry and enforcement authorities. The industry members have so far, however, failed to substantiate the claims they have made of illegal trading – unsurprisingly, hard evidence being somewhat difficult to come by. Specific allegations which have been investigated by customs authorities have usually failed to uncover proof of CFC smuggling. Nevertheless, circumstantial evidence continues to emerge, and given the extent of illegal trade in the US and in Asia, it would be quite surprising if none were occurring in Europe.

Sources and consumers

All the evidence suggests that Russia is a significant source of most of the illegally traded materials (see section 6.1). The Russian government has taken no serious actions to apply controls to its manufacturing sector, and hard currency earnings are a major temptation in an economy undergoing such dramatic convulsions. Individual plants may simply produce above their official quota, and sell the surplus on the black market. While the Russian government claimed production of 44,000 tonnes of ODS in 1994, and consumption of 33,000 tonnes,[200] external sources estimated a total

---

[198] Greene, 'The Montreal Protocol: implementation and development in 1995', p. 3.

[199] *New Scientist,* 19 March 1994, p. 6, cited in Greene, 'The Montreal Protocol', p. 3.

[200] UNEP, *Assessment of Basic Problems Confronting Countries with Economies in Transition in Complying with the Montreal Protocol: Report of the TEAP Ad-Hoc Working Group on CEIT Aspects,* November 1995, p. 24.

capacity of 100,000 tonnes,[201] with likely production possibly as high as 70,000 tonnes. Of seven known ODS production facilities, three are situated on military bases. Much of the material entering the US illegally is suspected of originating in Russia, and some at least has been trans-shipped through the UK.

Other sources include India (the source of the CFCs impounded in at least one of the successful US actions) and China (the source of illegal imports into Taiwan). ODS being sold in Asian markets below the normal retail price may be surplus illegal production from these sources. Both countries may experience difficulties in applying central controls to industrial plants – or may simply not wish to.

On the user side, it seems entirely likely that many purchasers, particularly small and medium-sized enterprises, simply are not aware of the illegal nature of their supplies; provision of advice to industry (probably most effectively organized in the US and UK) is always easiest to deliver to the largest users. Customs authorities have in general given a low priority to monitoring movements of ODS, particularly trans-shipments, and would benefit from additional training and awareness programmes. It has been suggested, for example, that some customs authorities are entirely unaware of the existence of any controls on the movements of ODS. Detection of the substances, which requires chemical analysis, is difficult, particularly if they are mislabelled; distinguishing adulterated virgin from genuine recycled material is virtually impossible.

The matter is of growing concern to the parties to the Montreal Protocol, as it clearly threatens the integrity of the phase-out schedules and the rate of recovery of the ozone layer. The topic was discussed at the Vienna Meeting; the Ozone Secretariat was requested to examine the information available to it on the issues of illegal imports and exports, dumping and uncontrolled production, and report back to the following year's Meeting.[202]

---

[201] Speech by Andrew Steer (Director, Environment Department, World Bank) to the Meeting of the Parties to the Montreal Protocol in Vienna, 5 December 1995.
[202] Decision VII/33 of the Parties to the Montreal Protocol.

6.3 Conclusion

The acceleration of the phase-out schedules through successive amendments to the Montreal Protocol has clearly speeded up the process of ozone layer recovery, and the rapid adoption by some countries of the amendments, together with the reinforcing trade provisions that come into effect subsequently, has encouraged other countries to participate. The process must not be so fast, however, that countries find themselves unable to comply with the accelerated phase-outs, and feel compelled to reinstate or expand domestic production, and/or turn to the black market for supplies. This is a fine balance to strike. So far, the parties to the Montreal Protocol appear to have achieved it, though the problem of non-compliance from Russia, a major producer of ODS, is a clear threat to the future of the ozone regime. It should also prompt a review of the effectiveness of the current non-compliance procedure.

On the issue of illegal trade, if an MEA is to place restrictions on the production and consumption of, and trade in, any particular substance, it is almost inevitable that a black market will appear. This is not a problem that environment ministries and international institutions can be expected to tackle by themselves, though they may need to be more active in a monitoring and detection capacity. It requires the cooperation and involvement of trade and industry ministries and enforcement agencies such as police and customs. The provision of financial and technical assistance to remove the problem at source is also an important factor in tackling illegal trade, as it is in tackling non-compliance. Conversion efforts in Russia, for instance, have so far focused almost exclusively on the phase-out of consumption, with relatively little attention paid to production. Concentrating on the latter as well would have the added benefit that closer monitoring of production would be required, leading to a much more accurate picture of the situation than has hitherto been possible.

Chapter 7

Conclusions and lessons for the future

The Montreal Protocol is generally recognized as one of the most success-ful multilateral environmental agreements – in the sense of achieving its objectives – yet negotiated. In concluding the paper, this chapter looks briefly at the lessons which can be learned from the experience of the Protocol, and particularly from its trade provisions and implications, for other prospective MEAs.

The Protocol owes its success to many factors, some of which are not necessarily repeatable in the context of future MEAs. These include, most importantly, the concentration of ODS production in a relatively small number of producers (17 companies), mostly in OECD countries, and, partly as a consequence, the small number of states involved in the origi-nal negotiations; the relatively easy availability of substitutes (though this was not originally anticipated); and the lack of any coherent and sustained industrial or public opposition. The timing of the issue, with the dramatic discovery of the hole in the Antarctic ozone layer in 1985, and the evi-dence of serious depletion revealed by the NASA expeditions in the late 1980s, coinciding with a period of economic upturn in Western economies, and accompanying general concern over the environment and 'quality of life' issues, was extremely propitious.

Many other factors may, however, be replicable. The progress of the negotiations in many ways provides a model for international treaty nego-tiation, fully involving participants from key groups such as business, sci-entists and NGOs. The flexibility built in to the Protocol in the form of its review process for targets and amendments has allowed continuous evolu-tion to meet changes in both scientific evidence and technological devel-opments. The limits on supply imposed by the control schedules encour-aged the rapid development of cost-effective alternatives which in turn helped to reduce demand, and the ability to trade production allowances in the interests of industrial rationalization provided an important element of flexibility. The recognition of the special needs of developing countries is crucial to the operation of any international agreement in a world comprising countries of widely varying incomes; this has taken the form of the provision of financial assistance and technology transfer, the decision-making procedures which allot particular weights to Article 5 countries, and the grace period before implementation of the phase-out schedules. Finally, the dynamic established by the progressively evolving phase-out schedules and the trade provisions has encouraged newly industrializing countries to move out of old technology and accelerate their own phase-outs even when not required to do so under the terms of the agreement.

The political climate may or may not be repeatable. Political considerations were in the end – and always will be – paramount (as in the choice of 50% for the initial phase-out target for CFCs, the outcome of political compromise rather than scientific reasoning). The negotiators' willingness to put the precautionary principle into effect, helped by relatively strong public opinion, plus the leadership role adopted initially by the US, and in recent years more often by the EU (particularly its northern members), were key factors.

The central feature of this paper has been a study of the trade provisions and impacts of the Montreal Protocol. To summarize:

- The trade provisions of the Protocol were a vital component in (a) building the wide international coverage it has achieved and (b) preventing industrial migration to non-parties to escape the controls on ODS.
- With regard to developing countries, the trade provisions were necessary but not sufficient for the effectiveness of the treaty; provision of financial support (through the Multilateral Fund) and technology transfer was also an essential element.
- Less GATT-inconsistent trade restrictions were not feasible. The problem of incompatibilities between the existing trade provisions and the GATT, although at this stage only a potential one, is nevertheless real. This both undermines the credibility of the ozone regime (since the trade restrictions have helped give industry the confidence it needed to

invest in alternatives to CFCs) and inhibits the negotiation of similar provisions in future MEAs.
- Problems have been caused for trade in ODS and in products containing ODS by the differential phase-out schedules of developing and industrialized countries.
- Illegal trade, and non-compliance by a major producer, pose threats to the goals of the treaty.

The experience of the Montreal Protocol suggests that future MEAs dealing with the control of substances causing transboundary environmental damage may find it necessary to incorporate trade provisions. The nature and effectiveness of these provisions will inevitably vary with the nature of the substances being controlled. In the case of climate change, for example, the range and volume of traded fuels and products is so huge as to make trade restrictions very difficult to negotiate and enforce. Conversely, of course, if they could be implemented effectively, they would provide a very powerful incentive to accede to the agreement, leading, as in the case of the Montreal Protocol, to near-universal participation.

Such trade restrictions in MEAs, like those of the Montreal Protocol, potentially violate the basic GATT principle of non-discrimination. They must therefore be both *legitimate* (they must be invoked for good reasons and must gain support from a wide and diverse range of countries) and *credible* (they must punish countries which do not cooperate and reward those which do).

In relation to such trade provisions, future MEAs (and, where relevant, the Montreal Protocol) should:

- Resolve the potential or actual incompatibilities between GATT and MEAs – preferably through an amendment to the GATT dealing with existing and future environmental agreements. The threat of possible action under the GATT should not be allowed to impede the negotiation of future MEAs.
- Anticipate the problems arising from trade between countries at different stages of implementation, including countries in non-compliance. Although developing countries clearly have a strong case for differential

treatment (depending on the topic of the MEA), the objectives of the treaty may be better achieved through relying on resource transfers rather than delays in implementation; if there are delays, they should be as short as possible. Licensing and monitoring systems covering trade in substances, products and technology may also prove valuable in helping to control the 'dumping' of obsolete products and technology in developing countries.

• Deal with the problem of illegal trade. If an MEA is to place restrictions on the production and consumption of, and trade in, any particular substance, it is almost inevitable that a black market will appear. Dealing with this requires coordinated action between trade and industry ministries and enforcement agencies such as police and customs as well as environment ministries and international institutions. The provision of financial and technical assistance to remove the problem at source is also an important factor in tackling illegal trade – and, indeed, non-compliance.

The objectives of trade liberalization and environmental sustainability are not mutually incompatible. The international community, however, does need to devise effective systems for ensuring that the pursuit of one does not prevent the achievement of the other. The negotiation and implementation of multilateral environmental agreements such as the Montreal Protocol offers the best way forward in striking the appropriate balance between trade and the environment – but only if questions and problems such as those outlined in this report are settled satisfactorily.